●●●architecture in context

First published 1997 by
Könemann Verlagsgesellschaft mbH
Bonner Straße 126
D–50968 Köln

ISBN 3–89508–271–6 Könemann

© 1997 Könemann Verlags-
gesellschaft mbH
Bonner Straße 126
D–50968 Köln

Published in Asia by
Page One Publishing Pte Ltd
Block 4 Pasir Panjang Road
#06-35 Alexandra Distripark
Singapore 118491

ISBN 981–00–8410–2

Published in the UK by
●●●ellipsis london limited
55 Charlotte Road
London EC2A 3QT

ISBN 1–899858–25–3 ellipsis

Designed and produced by
●●●ellipsis london limited

Photography by Keith Collie
Text by Peter Lloyd
Drawings by Micha Manz
Translated into German by
Andreas Klatt
Translated into French by
Armelle Tardiveau

Printed and bound in China

San Francisco ●●● architecture in context
Houses

after the fire

Peter Lloyd

photographs by

Keith Collie

●●●ellipsis KÖNEMANN

Introduction

An architectural fantasy – start with an enormous area of great natural beauty with wonderful views, add well-educated and affluent clients backed by millions of dollars of insurance-company money. Some of the most original architects working anywhere in the world are at hand. The conditions are ripe for an architectural experiment at an extraordinary scale.

In fact, while the rebuilding of the Oakland Hills fire zone has undoubtedly given rise to some innovative and thoughtful architecture, it also goes some way towards demonstrating what can go wrong when people get what they wished for. Traditional models, reused without any redeeming sense of irony, abound, testimony to the overwhelming power of cultural and technological conservatism.

Too many of the houses, financed by often-generous insurance payments, have bulked up like body builders. Square footage has become paramount and modest homes have swollen into grand houses, too close to their lot lines and to their neighbours, with too much house and not enough garden.

A few enlightened homeowners have commissioned architects whose work is unashamedly modern. (It should perhaps come as no surprise that the clients for the four modern houses featured in this book have careers or interests in the visual arts – as artists, photographers, graphic artists, collectors of and dealers in modern furniture.) These houses celebrate the pleasures of light and space and display frankly their structure and

materials. They could be seen as following in the tradition of the Southern Californian Case Study Houses – a series of experimental designs commissioned in the 1950s by John Entenza, owner and editor of <u>Arts & Architecture</u> magazine. The brief was to investigate ways of creating adventurous but inexpensive mass housing appropriate for the post-war United States, but what the programme actually produced was a number of imaginative one-off homes by architects including Richard Neutra, Ray and Charles Eames and Eero Saarinen, 23 of which were built. Stanley Saitowitz, architect of the McClane-Looke House, explicitly cites the Case Study Houses as a precedent, and certainly his building shares with designs such as Pierre Koenig's 1960 Case Study

House Number 22 a clarity of purpose, simplicity of construction, elision of interior and exterior, transparency and dynamism.

The fire in the hills above Oakland, to the east of San Francisco across the Bay Bridge, began on 20 October 1991. When the Hills were still uninhabited, fires during the fall season were regarded as part of a natural cycle of regeneration, but now their presence is no longer benign. Warm temperatures, high winds and five years of drought combined to make this autumn particularly dangerous. The fire, which started in an uninhabited area, soon established itself and quickly spread to cover 1800 acres. By the time it had been extinguished, it had destroyed nearly 3000 houses, killed 22 people and injured 148. The blaze became so fierce that walls of flame

1–2 Down the road is Frank Israel's quixotic Drager House. The flamboyant copper shield signals the drama of the interior with its interpenetrating floor levels and unexpected light wells.

1–2 Un peu plus bas se trouve la chimérique Drager House de Frank Israel. Le blason flamboyant en cuivre est précurseur de l'intérieur spectaculaire avec ses puits de lumière inattendus et dont les différents niveaux s'imbriquent.

1–2 Etwas weiter die Straße hinunter steht das kauzige Drager-Haus von Frank Israel. Die auffällige Kupfer-verkleidung signalisiert das Drama des Interieurs mit seinen ver-schachtelten Etagenebenen und unverhofften Lichtschächten.

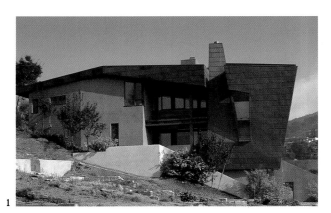

1

2

100 feet high swept across the dry hillsides and residents literally had to outrun the fire to survive. In the aftermath bodies were found in cars that had not been fast enough to escape the destruction.

The survivors lost everything. News camera crews spent days after the event filming shocked residents picking through the ruins of their homes, dumbfounded at the completeness of their loss, searching for any small reminder of their lives before the fire. Eighteen hundred houses and 900 apartment units were destroyed. Five thousand people were left homeless, with damage estimated at $2 billion.

The last two decades of the twentieth century have not been kind to California. A string of natural disasters – including the 1989 Loma Prieta earthquake that killed 63 people in San Francisco and the devastating 1994 earthquake in Los Angeles – has been paralleled by a series of political and racial infernos, most famously the 1992 LA riots that followed the televising of a home video of police beating black citizen Rodney King. Violent race relations coupled with economic recession have led to an exodus to states such as Arizona, Nevada, Florida and Washington, which offer economic incentives and a better quality of life. The Golden State has lost its gilt.

The hills of Oakland and Berkeley seem to have offered enough compensations for most of their inhabitants to take a second chance, however, and after the fire the area soon became a huge building site. How would this

3 The corner of Alvarado and Vicente demonstrates the diversity of architecture in the Hills. Among the unashamedly modern houses is a Maybeck house rebuilt almost to the original specifications.
4–5 Moore Ruble Yudell's Walrod House, located opposite the Maybeck reconstruction, is set back from the street and will soon begin to disappear modestly behind trees.

3 L'angle de Alvarado et de Vicente démontre la diversité architecturale des Oakland Hills. Parmi les maisons incroyablement modernes, on peut voir une maison réalisée par Maybeck reconstruite selon le cahier des charges d'origine.
4–5 La Walrod House de Moore Ruble Yudell, située face à la reconstruction de Maybeck, est en retrait de la rue et disparaîtra bientôt petit à petit derrière les feuilles des arbres.

3 Die Ecke Alvarado und Vicente stellt die Vielfältigkeit der Architektur in den Hills unter Beweis. Unter den unverhohlen modernen Gebäuden steht ein fast nach Originalentwürfen nachgebautes Maybeck-Haus.
4–5 Das Walrod-Haus von Moore Ruble Yudell, gegenüber der Maybeck-Rekonstruktion, ist von der Straße zurückgesetzt und wird bald bescheiden hinter Bäumen verschwinden.

3

4 5

sector of largely white, middle-class America choose to express its tastes, values and aspirations through that most American of building forms, the single-family home? Would complacency or anxiety dominate?

There is a strong trend in contemporary architecture in Europe, the United States and Japan for buildings that express the conflicts and dissonance, fragmentation and lack of a single, unchallenged voice of authority that are said to characterise the end of the twentieth century. In southern California, SCI-Arc (the Southern California Institute of Architecture) is the focus for a group of architects who express their distrust of modern society in their projects, from Morphosis to Eric Owen Moss and Frank Israel. Their sensibility owes a debt to LA

architect Frank Gehry, whose characteristic idiom combines commonplace materials such as corrugated metal (also used by Jim Jennings on the Becker House and Stanley Saitowitz on the McClane-Looke House), plywood, chain-link and asphalt in shocking, dissonant juxtapositions. One of Gehry's inspirations is the San Francisco-based artist David Ireland, whose Marin Center for the Arts involves a type of architectural archaeology whereby the layers of the building are stripped back and exposed.

One might have imagined that the Oakland Hills would be fertile ground for a full-blown architectural exploration of themes of alienation and disturbance, but this has not been the case. If the new buildings express a degree of unease, it is in subtle and

restrained ways. Of course, timber siding and shingles are now things of the past and the new structures are anchored to the bedrock by substantial concrete caissons, inviolable battleships of cement board and steel. But these are only sensible precautions against fire and earthquake, just as combustible trees such as eucalyptus have been replaced by fire-retardant planting such as agave. Recent social upheavals find expression in the fortress-like quality of many of the new homes, the tension between the desires to keep out intruders and to open living spaces to the climate and views. Security is obviously a prime consideration for most of these homeowners, though this is not unusual in largely white, suburban American enclaves. More fundamentally, the response to the

dangers already experienced and to the potential troubles ahead, whether natural, social or economic, has been to build on tradition, and almost any tradition with a pitched roof will do.

Californians and their near neighbours in Las Vegas have always paid scant attention to architectural conventions of time and place, so the notion of basing new buildings on loose interpretations of historical styles such as the popular Spanish Mission is not necessarily a retreat from the challenges of the present. The wave of eclecticism that swept Los Angeles in the 1920s gave rise to structures as shockingly inappropriate to their location as Grauman's Chinese Theater, the Mayan Theater, the Aztec Hotel and the mosque-like Girard Inn, while more recently Las Vegas has

1–2 David Baker and Associates' Kayo House gives the impression of a ramshackle, accretive building, with volumes apparently thrown together.
3 James Gillam's Laidley House takes its inspiration from the restraint of Japanese architecture and European modernism.

1–2 La Kayo House de David Baker and Associates, qui donne l'impression d'être délabrée, va en croissant avec ses deux volumes qui semblent être assemblés fortuitement.
3 La Laidley House de James Gilliam est inspirée de l'architecture sobre japonaise et de l'architecture moderniste européenne.

1–2 Das Kayo-Haus von David Baker und Associates vermittelt den Eindruck von morscher Zu-fälligkeit, wahllos zusammen-gewürfelt.
3 Das Laidley-Haus von James Gillam orientiert sich an den Zwängen japanischer Architektur und des europäischen Moder-nismus.

1

2

Le rêve en architecture, c'est un immense espace d'une beauté naturelle extraordinaire, un maître d'ouvrage riche et cultivé qui a perçu des millions de dollars de compagnies d'assurances et des architectes, parmi les plus originaux du monde, à disposition. Les conditions sont alors réunies pour réaliser une architecture hors du commun à très grande échelle.

La reconstruction du secteur des Oakland Hills, dévastée par l'incendie de 1991, a, d'une part, permis l'émergence d'une architecture innovatrice et pensée jusque dans les moindres détails et, d'autre part, a mis à nu des erreurs d'une architecture réalisée selon la volonté des maîtres d'ouvrage. Les modèles traditionnels, remâchés et dépourvus de tout humour,

spawned hotel/casinos modelled after an Egyptian pyramid and a tropical rainforest. San Francisco offers delights such as the old Alcazar Theater on Geary Street, an ornately decorated, Islamic-style structure designed in 1917 by T. Patterson Ross, or Joseph Leonard's flamboyant building of 1905 at 2963 Webster Street with its roofscape of crenellations, Russian domes and Chinese pagodas. Each offers proof that ideas of time and place – or of what a building should be – are permeable. Cultural and architectural history can be rehashed to produce new hybrids; houses can become narratives or riddles, explainable by reference not to site or materials but to stories and ideas – as with maverick ACE Architects' recent Oakland building allegedly inspired by a fictional battle between a sea monster and a supertanker.

The Bay Area's tradition of architectural innovation has been categorised by historians as having three distinct phases. The most imposing figure of the first phase, Bernard Maybeck (1862–1957), combines a pre-modernist interest in structural experimentation and use of materials with a West Coast eclecticism. His First Church of Christ, Scientist in Berkeley (1910), for which he used prefabricated units, was at the same time a blend of styles and technologies that almost defies description. Gothic tracery and romanesque piers are cast in concrete; windows have factory steel sashes; exterior walls are clad in asbestos panels (a distant relation to the cement board used by Mark

abondent et témoignent de l'emprise du pouvoir conservateur, tant culturel que technologique. On a érigé trop de maisons cossues, financées par les indemnités de compagnies d'assurances, bien souvent généreuses. La surface au sol est devenue le critère primordial et les petites maisons ont pris tant de volume qu'elles touchent les limites de leur terrain et les habitations voisines. La taille des maisons est devenue disproportionnée par rapport à celle de leur jardin.

Quelques propriétaires bien inspirés ont engagé des architectes dont les réalisations sont résolument modernes. (Il n'est pas étonnant que les maîtres d'ouvrage des quatre maisons présentées dans ce livre travaillent dans le domaine des arts. Ils

sont artistes, photographes, graphistes, collectionneurs ou marchands de meubles contemporains). Ces maisons célèbrent les plaisirs de la lumière et de l'espace et exposent clairement leur structure ainsi que les matériaux employés. On peut les apprécier comme un héritage de l'époque des Southern Californian Case Study Houses – une étude de conceptions expérimentales pour habitation commandée dans les années 50 par John Entenza, propriétaire et éditeur du magazine <u>Arts & Architecture</u>. Le programme consistait en une étude sur de nouvelles façons de construire des logements en série qui soient à la fois originaux, bon marché et adaptés au contexte économique de l'après-guerre. Pour finir, ce sont des maisons uniques et très imaginatives – conçues par des architectes

tels que Richard Neutra, Ray et Charles Eames ou Eero Saarinen – qui ont émergé de cette recherche et 23 d'entre elles ont été construites.

Stanley Saitowitz, l'architecte de la McClane-Looke House, cite en exemple l'étude lancée par John Entenza et on peut noter les caractéristiques communes de sa maison avec l'étude n° 22 de Pierre Koenig, conçue en 1960, quant à la clarté d'intention, la simplicité dans la construction, l'élision de l'intérieur et de l'extérieur, la transparence et le dynamisme.

Le 20 octobre 1991, l'incendie s'est déclaré dans les collines au dessus de Oakland, situé à l'est de San Francisco, de l'autre côté de Bay Bridge. A l'époque où ces collines étaient encore inhabitées, les

incendies d'automne faisaient partie du cycle naturel de la régénération des terres mais, aujourd'hui, ils ne sont plus un phénomène mineur. La chaleur, les vents forts et cinq années consécutives de sécheresse ont créé un terrain particulièrement dangereux. L'incendie, qui a commencé dans une zone inhabitée, s'est rapidement propagé sur plus de 3 600 hectares, détruisant plus de 3 000 maisons, faisant 148 blessés et causant la mort de 22 personnes. La violence du feu était telle que des murs de flammes d'une hauteur de 30 mètres balayaient les flans des collines, si bien que pour survivre les résidents n'avaient d'autres solutions que de courir au devant du feu. Plus tard, on a retrouvé des voitures avec les corps calcinés des gens qui n'avaient

3

Horton on the House on a Hilltop and by Jim Jennings on the Becker House, now a common material thanks to the need for fireproofing); roofs with heavy eaves are almost Chinese in style, while the desire to link the building to the landscape by means of pergolas and trellises is pure California. Maybeck also produced a line of domestic architecture influenced initially by the indigenous buildings of the Bay Area: simple wood-framed and shingled houses half hidden by trees. More characteristic, however, is the ambitious Hearst Hall (1899) with its gothic arches of laminated wood, the first of their kind. Hearst Hall, which burned down in 1922, is reflected strongly in the Jordan House by ACE Architects, who no doubt enjoyed the irony of replacing a burned-down building

with a near copy of another burned-down building. In the rebuilding that followed the major San Francisco earthquake of 1906, Maybeck explored techniques and materials that would withstand fire and seismic forces, using concrete for the first time in the Lawson House in Berkeley in 1907.

The second phase of the Bay Area tradition includes the work of William Wurster (1895–1973), who was active from the 1920s to the 1960s. His Gregory Farmhouse in Santa Cruz (1927), with its low, ranch-style buildings opening on to a continuous verandah and arranged around a courtyard, was disapprovingly labelled 'carpenter' or 'shanty' style, though Wurster himself insisted that his work was simply a response to location and programme. Parallels can be

drawn between the Gregory Farmhouse and Fernau and Hartman's recent Berggruen House, a collection of agricultural-type sheds strung out over a wooded site, or Gehry's Schnabel House in Los Angeles (1989), with its village-like grouping of volumes. One of Wurster's most unexpected buildings is the Pope House Number 2 in Orinda (1940), constructed of concrete block and corrugated-metal sheet and dominated by a central courtyard that could be enclosed by large sliding doors or opened to the view. The use of materials and 'tail', like the crest of a wave, are reminiscent of Saitowitz's McLane-Looke House.

Like Maybeck before them, second-phase Bay Area architects such as Joseph Esherick, John Dinwiddie and John Funk explored new

technologies in ways appropriate to northern California. Dinwiddie's Roos House in San Francisco (1938) and Funk's Woerner House in Marin County (1948) make reference to the architecture of Le Corbusier and Mies van der Rohe respectively, but rendered in materials common to the Bay Area. Their work could perhaps best be described as 'regional modernism'.

The 1960s work of Charles Moore, in partnership with Lyndon Turnbull Whitaker, belongs to the Bay Area tradition's third phase. For projects such as Sea Ranch, north of San Francisco, Moore drew inspiration from the vernacular simplicity of the traditional wooden California barn and the spartan rigour he found in the work of Louis Kahn. Moore's former partner

pas été assez rapides pour échapper à la catastrophe.

Les survivants ont tout perdu. Les équipes de télévision ont filmé des journées durant les habitants en état de choc et anéantis face à l'ampleur des dégâts à la recherche de souvenirs leur rappelant leur vie avant l'incendie. Mille huit cents maisons et 900 appartements ont été détruits. Cinq mille personnes se sont retrouvées sans logement et les dégâts sont estimés à quelque 2 milliards de dollars.

La Californie n'a pas été épargnée au cours des deux dernières décennies du XXème siècle. Elle a subit une série de catastrophes naturelles – notamment le tremblement de terre de Loma Prieta en 1989 qui a fait 63 victimes et celui de Los Angeles

Der Traum jedes Architekten: Man nehme ein riesiges Areal von großer landschaftlicher Schönheit, mit herrlichen Ausblicken, dazu gebildete und wohlhabende Klienten, die auf eine Finanzierung durch Versicherungsgelder in Millionenhöhe zurückgreifen können. Einige der genialsten Architekten der Welt stehen zur Verfügung. Die Bedingungen für ein architektonisches Experiment ungeheurer Größenordnung sind damit gegeben.

In Wirklichkeit hat zwar die Sanierung der Brandzone Oakland Hills zweifelsohne einiges an innovativer und gut durchdachter Architektur hervorgebracht, aber sie hat auch gezeigt, was schiefgehen kann, wenn man genau das bekommt, was man sich gewünscht hat. Die Vielzahl an herkömmlichen Modellen, die ohne jeden ausgleichenden Sinn für Ironie

recycelt wurden, zeugt von der überwältigenden Macht des kulturellen und technologischen Konservatismus. Zu viele Häuser, deren Bau durch oftmals großzügige Versicherungsgelder finanziert wurde, lassen massig die Muskeln spielen. Der Grundfläche wurde höchste Priorität eingeräumt, und aus bescheidenen Wohnhäusern wurden Prunkbauten mit zu wenig Abstand zur Grenze des Grundstücks oder zum Nachbarhaus – wobei dem Zuviel an Haus nicht genug Garten gegenübersteht.

Einige wenige aufgeklärte Hausbesitzer haben Architekten beauftragt, die sich mit ihren Arbeiten ganz unverhohlen modern geben. (Dabei überrascht es vielleicht nicht, daß die Bauherren der vier in diesem Buch geschilderten Häuser in den darstellenden

Künsten tätig sind, oder wenigstens ein Interesse daran haben – als Künstler, Fotografen, Grafiker, Sammler und Händler moderner Möbel.) Diese Häuser zelebrieren die Freuden von Licht und Raum und versuchen nicht, ihre Struktur und Baumaterialien zu kaschieren. Man kann sie in die Tradition der »Southern Californian Case Study Houses« einordnen; dabei handelte es sich um eine Reihe von experimentellen Entwürfen, die in den 50er Jahren von John Entenza, dem Besitzer und Herausgeber der Zeitschrift Arts & Architecture in Auftrag gegeben wurden. Die Aufgabe lautete, Möglichkeiten zum Bau gewagter, aber zugleich preiswerter, den Nachkriegsgegebenheiten in den USA angemessener Häuser für den allgemeinen Wohnungsbedarf zu finden. Das Programm

William Turnbull continues to practise in the Bay Area: his recent Foothill Student Housing in Berkeley uses vernacular forms and wooden structural and cladding elements and displays a quirky sense of proportion similar to that of Moore.

The history of the fourth phase of the Bay Area tradition has yet to be written, though it seems apparent already that it is less easy to define than its predecessors. If the clash of new houses by Moore Ruble Yudell, Saitowitz, Frank Israel and James Gillam at the corner of Alvarado and Vicente in the fire zone is anything to go by, perhaps its only salient characteristic is a sensitivity to site. Because of the fire, the architects of the new homes in the Hills can design without neighbouring buildings to consider, without trees and

en 1994, d'autant plus dévastateur – et parallèlement, une série d'émeutes politiques et raciales, dont la plus retentissante est celle de 1992 à Los Angeles suite à la diffusion d'une vidéo montrant la police en train de passer à tabac Rodney King, un citoyen noir. Les relations violentes entre les populations de couleurs différentes ajoutées à la crise économique ont entraîné un exode vers d'autres États tels que l'Arizona, le Nevada, la Floride et l'État de Washington dont la situation économique et la qualité de vie sont meilleures. La Californie a perdu tous ses attraits.

Après l'incendie, la plupart des résidents des collines de Oakland et de Berkeley ont perçu des indemnités suffisamment importantes pour, malgré tout, recommencer

à zéro et rapidement tranformer les collines en un immense chantier. Ce quartier allait-il prendre forme selon les goûts, les valeurs et les aspirations d'une population principalement blanche et de classe moyenne et voir s'édifier des maisons familiales individuelles, la construction américaine par excellence ? Entre la suffisance et la paranoïa, quel aspect allait-il dominer ?

En Europe, aux États Unis et au Japon, il existe un courant très important, en architecture contemporaine, pour la construction de bâtiments qui expriment les conflits et la discordance, la fragmentation et l'absence d'une norme établie et indiscutée qui, dit-on, caractérisent cette fin de siècle. L'école d'architecture SCI-Arc (Southern California Institute of Architecture) du sud de

la Californie est le centre d'un groupe d'architectes, tels que Morphosis, Eric Owen Moss ou Frank Israel, qui expriment dans leurs projets une méfiance à l'égard de la société moderne. Ils puisent leur inspiration auprès de Frank Gehry, un architecte de Los Angeles, dont le vocabulaire caractéristique est un assemblage et une juxtaposition, à la fois choquante et discordante, de matériaux ordinaires comme les métaux ondulés (que l'on retrouve dans la Becker House de Jim Jennings ou dans la McClane-Looke House de Stanley Saitowitz), le contre-plaqué, le maillon de chaîne et l'asphalte. L'une des sources d'inspiration de Frank Gehry est l'artiste David Ireland, établi à San Francisco, dont le centre pour les arts (Marin Center for the Arts) consiste en une sorte d'archéologie

architecturale qui expose et met à nu les diverses couches du bâtiment.

On aurait pu imaginé que Oakland Hills serait un terrain propice à l'expérimentation architecturale grandeur nature aux thèmes d'aliénation et de confusion, mais il n'en a rien été. Si les nouvelles constructions expriment un certain malaise ce n'est que de façon très subtile et timide. Bien sûr, on a remplacé les traditionnels bardages en bois et les essentes par des structures que de solides caissons en béton ancrent à la base. Ces structures sont de véritables cuirassés inviolables, aux platelages en ciment et acier. Ce ne sont là que des mesures de protection pratiques contre les incendies et les tremblements de terre, tout comme le remplacement des eucalyptus, un bois

brachte letztlich jedoch etwas ganz anderes hervor, nämlich eine Reihe von einfallsreichen Einzelentwürfen von Architekten wie Richard Neutra, Ray und Charles Eames und Eero Saarinen, von denen 23 realisiert wurden. Stanley Saitowitz, der Architekt des McClane-Looke-Hauses, nennt ausdrücklich die Case-Study-Häuser als Vorläufer, und sein Gebäude ist eindeutig mit dem 1960 von Pierre Koenig erbauten Case Study House Nr. 22 vergleichbar, was klare Zweckbestimmung, einfache Konstruktion, Elision von Interieur und Exterieur, Transparenz und Dynamik angeht.

Das Feuer in den Bergen oberhalb von Oakland, östlich von San Francisco auf der anderen Seite der Bay-Brücke, brach am 20. Oktober 1991 aus. Als die Berge noch unbesiedelt waren, galten Flächenbrände im

Herbst als Teil eines natürlichen Regenerationszyklus, doch inzwischen sind sie für den Menschen gefährlich geworden. Durch das Zusammenwirken hoher Temperaturen, starker Winde und einer fünfjährigen Dürre war die Gefahr in dem betreffenden Herbst besonders groß. Das Feuer, das auf unbesiedeltem Gelände ausbrach, griff schnell um sich und hatte bald ein Gebiet von fast 730 ha erfaßt. Als es endlich gelang, den Brand zu löschen, hatte er fast 3 000 Häuser zerstört, 22 Menschenleben gefordert und 148 Personen verletzt. Zeitweise rasten Flammenwände von über 30 Metern Höhe über die Berghänge, und die Anwohner waren gezwungen, vor den Flammen die Flucht zu ergreifen. Später fand man Tote in Autos, die nicht schnell genug gewesen waren.

Die Überlebenden verloren alles. Tagelang filmten die Nachrichten-Crews vom Fernsehen die geschockten Anwohner, die in den Ruinen ihrer Häuser herumstocherten. Sie waren durch den totalen Verlust wie benommen und suchten nach einer noch so kleinen Erinnerung an ihr Leben vor dem Brand. 1 800 Häuser und 900 Wohnungen wurden zerstört. 5 000 Menschen wurden obdachlos. Der Sachschaden belief sich auf schätzungsweise zwei Milliarden Dollar.

Das auslaufende 20. Jahrhundert ist für Kalifornien keine gute Zeit gewesen. Neben einer Reihe von Naturkatastrophen – darunter das Erdbeben von 1989 in Loma Prieta, bei dem 63 Menschen ums Leben kamen, und das verheerende Erdbeben von 1994 in Los Angeles – kam es auch zu einer Serie von

vegetation to work around, with none of the usual limitations to struggle against except the stringencies of the building codes. The houses they are replacing had to fit into an established architectural and planted landscape; the new homes have none, except for memories. What they do have is a bare site, a glorious location, and the opportunity to develop a programme in close collaboration with the client.

Each of the houses featured in this book shares a concern for making controlled spaces in which a programme for living is expressed with extreme clarity. In contrast with many of the new houses in the Hills, these buildings employ a language of some delicacy, using screens, reflective materials and structure to break up their bulk. These

houses are risky: even seen from a distance, they assert their individuality. Yet they are also purposeful and simple, with a simplicity learned from the great tradition – as real as the traditions of Spanish Colonial or Tudorbethan eclecticism – of modernism. Where so many of the new houses in the Hills content themselves with reproducing a vocabulary from the past in an unoriginal manner, these buildings extend the principles of modernism to produce an architecture appropriate to West Coast life at the end of the twentieth century.

1 ACE Architects' Cotten House, designed for an enthusiastic horn player, was inspired by the remains of a saxophone found in the ruins of the old house.
2 ACE Architects' Jordan House is a distant reflection of Maybeck's Hearst Hall, which burned down in 1922. No doubt the architects enjoyed the irony of replacing a burned building with a design based on a burned building.

1 La Cotten House de ACE Architects, conçue pour un joueur de cor passioné, est inspirée des restes d'un saxophone trouvé dans les décombres de l'ancienne maison.
2 La Jordan House de ACE Architects est un vague écho au Hearst Hall de Maybeck qui a brûlé en 1922. A n'en pas douter, les architectes se sont amusés à l'idée de remplacer une maison brûlée par la copie d'une construction elle aussi brûlée.

1 Das für einen passionierten Horn-spieler entstandene Cotten-Haus von ACE Architects verdankt seine Inspiration einem Saxophon, das man in den Ruinen des alten Gebäudes fand.
2 Im Jordan-Haus von ACE Archi-tects hallt die Erinnerung an ein bereits 1922 abgebranntes Gebäude von Maybeck nach: Hearst Hall. Zweifellos wußten die Archi-tekten die Ironie zu schätzen.

1

combustible, par des arbres tels que l'agave qui freinent l'incendie.

Les récents soulèvements sociaux ont entraîné la construction de maisons-forteresses dont la conception est tiraillée entre la volonté de tenir les intrus à l'écart et celle de créer des espaces de vie ouverts au paysage environnant. Pour la plupart des propriétaires, la sécurité est bien entendu primordiale – ce qui n'est d'ailleurs pas une exigence inabituelle dans les enclaves américaines suburbaines dont la population prédominante est blanche. Mais, plus fondamentalement, la réponse aux dangers déjà vécus et aux troubles susceptibles de se produire, qu'ils soient d'origine naturelle, sociale ou économique, est de construire selon la tradition et toute tradition fait

verhängnisvollen politischen und rassen-politischen Konflikten. So brachen 1992 in Los Angeles Bürgerunruhen aus, nachdem im Fernsehen ein Amateurvideo gesendet wurde, das zeigte, wie ein schwarzer Bürger, Rodney King, von der Polizei zusammengeschlagen worden war. Die Gewalt zwischen ethnischen Gruppen und eine Konjunkturflaute haben zur Abwanderung nach Staaten wie Arizona, Nevada, Florida und Washington geführt, die wirtschaftliche Anreize und eine bessere Lebensqualität bieten. Der »Golden State« hat seinen Glanz eingebüßt.

Doch die Berge von Oakland und Berkeley sind offenbar reizvoll genug, um die meisten der Bewohner zum Bleiben zu bewegen. Schon bald nach dem Brand verwandelte sich das Gebiet in eine riesige Baustelle. Wie würde

dieser Bevölkerungsteil, der sich vorwiegend aus weißen Amerikanern der Mittelklasse zusammensetzte, seinen Geschmack, seine Werte und Ansprüche durch eine so typisch amerikanische Bauform wie das Einfamilien-haus zum Ausdruck bringen? Würde Selbst-gefälligkeit oder Ängstlichkeit die Oberhand gewinnen?

Es gibt in der zeitgenössischen Architektur Europas, der Vereinigten Staaten und Japans einen starken Trend hin zu Gebäuden, in denen die Konflikte und Dissonanzen, die Fragmentierung und das Fehlen einer defini-tiven, unangefochtenen Autorität zum Aus-druck kommen – alles Elemente, die als typisch für die letzten Jahre des 20. Jahr-hunderts gelten. In Südkalifornien hat sich in SCI-Arc (südkalifornisches Institut für

Architektur) eine Gruppe von Architekten zusammengefunden, die ihr Mißtrauen gegen-über der modernen Gesellschaft in ihren Pro-jekten kundtun, von Morphosis bis zu Eric Owen Moss und Frank Israel. Den Sinn dafür verdanken sie zum Teil dem in Los Angeles tätigen Architekten Frank Gehry, dessen charakteristische Ausdrucksweise gängige Materialien wie Wellblech (auch von Jim Jennings für das Becker-Haus und von Stanley Saitowitz beim McClane-Looke-Haus ver-wendet), Sperrholz, Drahtgeflecht und Asphalt in schockierender, dissonanter Gegenüber-stellung beinhaltet. Gehry wurde unter an-derem von dem in San Francisco lebenden Künstler David Ireland inspiriert, der in seinem Kunstzentrum Marin Center for the Arts eine Art von architektonischer Archäo-

2

l'affaire dès l'instant qu'elle comprend un toit en pente.

Les Californiens et leurs voisins de Las Vegas n'ont jamais porté grande attention aux conventions architecturales de temps et d'espace. Par conséquent, l'idée de créer de nouvelles constructions en s'inspirant plus ou moins des styles historiques (par exemple, le très populaire «Spanish Mission») ne signifie pas nécessairement un retour en arrière face aux défis conceptuels d'aujourd'hui. La vague d'éclectisme, qui a balayé Los Angeles dans les années 20, a donné lieu à des structures à la fois choquantes et inadaptées au site. On peut citer le Grauman's Chinese Theater, le Mayan Theater, l'Aztec Hotel et le Girard Inn (qui ressemble à une mosquée) et, plus récemment, les hôtels-casinos de Las Vegas

qui sont conçus sur les thèmes des pyramides égyptiennes ou des forêts tropicales. De son côté San Francisco offre des merveilles telles que le vieil Alcazar Theater sur Geary Street, une construction dans un style islamique surchargée d'ornements réalisée en 1917 par T. Patterson Ross, ou encore le flamboyant bâtiment sis au 2963 Webster Street, conçu par Joseph Leonard en 1905, dont la ligne du toit est ponctuée de créneaux, de dômes à la russe et de pagodes à la chinoise. Chacun de ces bâtiments démontre que la conception de temps et de lieu – ou de ce qu'un bâtiment devrait être – est très flexible. L'histoire culturelle et architecturale est ainsi revue et corrigée pour créer de nouveaux hybrides. Les maisons sont alors des récits ou des devinettes qui s'expliquent non pas en

fonction du site ou des matériaux mais en fonction des histoires et des idées – tel est le cas de la construction réalisée récemment à Oakland par l'agence avant-gardiste ACE qui s'est inspirée d'une bataille fictive entre un monstre des mers et un pétrolier géant.

Les historiens distinguent trois périodes dans la tradition d'innovation architecturale autour de la Baie de San Francisco. Bernard Maybeck (1862–1957), personnage prédominant de la première période, associe un intérêt pré-moderne à l'expérimentation des structures et à l'utilisation de matériaux dont l'éclectisme est typique de la Côte Ouest. Son église, First Church of Christ, Scientist à Berkeley (1910), conçue avec des unités préfabriquées, est un mélange de styles et de technologies presque impossible

à décrire. Les dentelles gothiques et les piliers romans sont en béton, les fenêtres sont pourvues de châssis à guillotines d'usine en acier, les murs sont revêtus de panneaux en amiante (qui rappellent vaguement les panneaux de ciment utilisés par Mark Horton dans la House on a Hilltop et la Becker House de Jim Jennings et qui sont aujourd'hui des matériaux courants en raison de la nécessité d'ignifugation), enfin les toits sont dotés de grands avant-toits à la chinoise. Par ailleurs, il y a le désir typiquement californien d'intégrer le bâtiment au paysage au moyen de pergolas et de treillages. Maybeck a aussi produit un style d'architecture familial inspiré des maisons indigènes de la Baie de San Francisco dont l'ossature simple en bois est essentée et qui sont en partie cachées

logie verwirklicht hat, bei der einzelne Lagen des Gebäudes herausgeschält und freigelegt werden.

Man möchte meinen, daß in den Bergen oberhalb Oaklands der Gedanke, die Thematik der Verfremdung und Unruhe architektonisch aufzuarbeiten, auf fruchtbaren Boden gefallen wäre, aber dem war nicht so. Die neuen Gebäude bringen zwar ein gewisses Maß an Unruhe zum Ausdruck, aber nur auf subtile und verhaltene Weise. Holzverkleidung und -schindeln gehören selbstverständlich der Vergangenheit an, und die neuen Bauten sind durch gewaltige Beton-Caissons fest im Grundgestein verankert – unantastbare Schlachtschiffe aus Betonplatten und Stahl. Aber das sind nur vernünftige Vorsichtsmaßnahmen gegen Brände oder Erdbeben.

Auch die leicht flammbaren Bäume wie der Eukalyptus wurden durch feuerhemmende Pflanzungen von z. B. Agaven ersetzt. Die sozialen Umwälzungen der jüngsten Zeit spiegeln sich in dem festungsähnlichen Aussehen vieler der neuen Wohnhäuser wider, in der Spannung zwischen dem Wunsch, Eindringlinge fernzuhalten, und dem Bedürfnis, offene Wohnräume zu haben, um Klima und Aussicht zu genießen. Die Sicherheit ist ganz offensichtlich für die meisten Hausbesitzer ein vordringliches Thema, obwohl das in vorwiegend weißen Vorstadtenklaven der USA keine Seltenheit ist. Wesentlicher ist die Tatsache, daß man auf bereits erlebte und potentielle künftige Gefahren, ob aus der Natur, der Gesellschaft oder dem Wirtschaftsleben, mit Traditionsbewußtsein reagierte,

wobei fast jede Tradition den Ansprüchen genügt, solange sie ein Giebeldach hat.

Die Kalifornier und ihre Nachbarn im nahe gelegenen Las Vegas haben sich nie sonderlich um die geographischen und historischen Konventionen der Architektur geschert; die Idee, sich mit einem neuen Gebäude an eine lockere Interpretation einer historischen Stilrichtung, wie z. B. des beliebten Spanish-Mission-Stils, zu halten, muß nicht unbedingt als Absage an die Herausforderungen der Gegenwart gesehen werden. Die Welle des Eklektizismus, die sich in den 20er Jahren in Los Angeles ausbreitete, brachte Bauwerke hervor, die in Anbetracht der örtlichen Gegebenheiten so unangemessen sind, daß sie geradezu schockieren: Grauman's Chinese Theater zum Beispiel, das

1 2

1–2 Savidge Warren Fillinger's Schmid
House uses steel and cement board
in a strictly organised design that
relies on the repetition of a module
and standard components.

3–4 The modest single-storey streetside
elevation of Burks Toma's House
on Besito Avenue gives way
to a swaggering battleship of
perforated steel awnings, balconies
and angled sections plunging five
levels down the hillside.

1–2 L'acier et des panneaux de ciment
sont les matériaux utilisés pour
la Schmid House de Savidge
Warren Fillinger dont le design
très rigoureux est fondé sur
la répétition d'un module et
d'éléments standard.

3–4 L'élévation sans prétention d'un
étage, côté rue, de la maison
réalisée par Burks Toma et située
sur Besito Avenue fait place à un
bâtiment qui ressemble à un navire
fanfaronnant fait de tauds en
aluminium perforé, de balcons et
de profilés coudés sur une hauteur
de cinq étages le long de la colline.

1–2 Das Schmid-Haus von Savidge
Warren Fillinger arbeitet mit Stahl
und Betonplatten in einem streng
angelegten Entwurf, der sich auf
die Wiederholung eines Moduls
und Standardelemente stützt.

3–4 Hinter der bescheidenen ein-
stöckigen Straßenfassade des
Hauses an der Besito Avenue
von Burks Toma verbirgt sich
ein forsches Schlachtschiff mit
Sonnensegeln aus perforierten
Stahlblechen, Balkonen und ab-
gewinkelten Sektionen in fünf
Geschossen am Hang.

Mayan Theater, das Aztec Hotel und das an
eine Moschee erinnernde Girard Inn. Gerade
in jüngster Zeit wurden in Las Vegas Hotel-
kasinos errichtet, die sich eine ägyptische
Pyramide oder einen tropischen Regenwald
zum Vorbild nehmen. San Francisco bietet an
solchen Genüssen zum Beispiel das alte Alcazar Theatre auf der Geary Street, ein prunk-
voll geschmücktes Gebäude im islamischen
Stil, das 1917 von T. Patterson Ross entwor-
fen wurde, und das 1905 entstandene, extra-
vagante Bauwerk von Joseph Leonard, 2963
Webster Street, mit seiner zinnenbesetzten
Dachlandschaft, russischen Zwiebeltürmen
und chinesischen Pagoden. Jedes dieser
Werke liefert den Beweis, daß Vorstellungen
über Zeit und Ort – oder darüber, was ein
Gebäude zu sein hat – fließend sind. Kultur-

und Architekturgeschichte lassen sich beliebig neu aufbereiten, um neue Hybridformen
hervorzubringen; Häuser können Geschichten
erzählen oder zu Rätseln werden, die nicht
durch einen Verweis auf den Ort oder die
Materialien, sondern nur über Geschichten
und Ideen aufzuschlüsseln sind – wie etwa ein
neueres Gebäude der Außenseiter-Firma ACE
Architects in Oakland, das von einer fiktiven
Schlacht zwischen einem Seeungeheuer und
einem Supertanker inspiriert wurde.

Die in der Bay Area vorherrschende In-
novationsfreudigkeit in der Architektur wird
von Historikern in drei deutlich getrennte
Phasen eingeteilt. Der renommierteste Ver-
treter der ersten Phase, Bernard Maybeck
(1862-1957), verband ein prämoderni-
stisches Interesse an strukturellen Experi-

menten und der Materialverwendung mit dem
für die amerikanische Westküste typischen
Eklektizismus. Bei seiner First Church of
Christ, Scientist in Berkeley (1910), für die
er vorgefertigte Teile verwendete, vermischte
er in nahezu unbeschreiblicher Weise die
unterschiedlichsten Stile und Technologien.
Gotisches Maßwerk und romanische Pfeiler
wurden in Beton gegossen; Schiebefenster
sind aus Industriestahl gefertigt; die Außen-
wände sind mit Asbestplatten verkleidet (ent-
fernte Verwandte der Betonplatten, die von
Mark Horton für das »House on a Hilltop« und
von Jim Jennings beim Becker-Haus gewählt
wurden; heute aus feuerschutztechnischen
Gründen ein häufig anzutreffendes Material);
die Dächer mit ihren schweren Traufen wirken
vom Stil her fast chinesisch, während der

3　4

par des arbres. Mais l'ambitieux Hearst
Hall (1899) reste la réalisation la plus
caractéristique de son oeuvre avec
l'utilisation, pour la première fois, de contre-
plaqué pour des voûtes gothiques. On
retrouve le style du Hearst Hall, qui a brûlé
en 1922, dans la Jordan House de ACE
Architects qui, à n'en pas douter, se sont
amusés à l'idée de remplacer une maison
brûlée par la copie d'une autre construction
brûlée. Dans le processus de reconstruction
de San Francisco qui a suivi le tremblement
de terre de 1922, Maybeck a étudié les
techniques et les matériaux résistant au feu
et aux secousses sismiques et a fait usage
du béton, pour la première fois, dans la
construction de la Lawson House de Berkeley
en 1907.

La seconde période de la Baie de San
Francisco comprend les réalisations de
William Wurster (1895–1973) dont le travail
s'étend des années 20 aux années 60.
La Gregory Farmhouse à Santa Cruz (1927)
– dont la construction peu élevée, typique
des ranchs, se prolonge sur une véranda
attenante et s'organise autour d'une cour –
fut sévèrement critiquée et qualifiée de style
«charpentier» et de «bicoque». Wurster a
justifié son choix en fonction des exigences
du site et du programme. On peut comparer
la Gregory Farmhouse à la Berggruen House,
récemment réalisée par Fernau et Hartman et
qui consiste en une succession de structures
de type rural qui s'étendent sur un site boisé,
ainsi qu'à la Schnabel House à Los Angeles
(1989) de Frank Gehry dont le regroupement

des volumes s'organise comme ceux d'un
village. La Pope House Number 2 à Orinda
(1940) est certainement l'une des maisons
les plus inattendues de Wurster. Faite de
blocs en béton et feuilles en métal ondulé, sa
caractéristique principale est la cour centrale
que l'on peut soit fermer à l'aide d'immenses
portes coulissantes soit ouvrir sur le paysage
alentour. L'utilisation de matériaux et de
la «queue», comme la crête d'une vague,
rappelle la McLane-Looke House de Saitowitz.

Tout comme Maybeck avant eux, les
architectes de la seconde période de la Baie
de San Francisco tels que Joseph Esherick,
John Dinwiddie et John Funk ont étudié de
nouveaux moyens technologiques adaptés à
la Californie du Nord. La Roos House à San
Francisco (1938) de Dinwiddie et la Woerner

House à Marin County (1948) de Funk sont
respectivement inspirées de l'architecture de
Le Corbusier et de Mies van der Rohe mais
sont revêtues de matériaux typiques de la
Baie. On pourrait qualifier leur travail de
«modernisme régional».

Les réalisations de Charles Moore dans les
années 60, qui était alors associé à Lyndon
Tunbull Whitaker, représentent la troisième
période de la tradition de la Baie de San
Francisco. Pour des projets comme celui
du Sea Ranch au nord de San Francisco,
Moore s'est inspiré de la simplicité de la
traditionnelle grange en bois californienne
et de la rigueur spartiate que l'on retrouve
dans l'œuvre de Louis Kahn. William Turnbull,
l'ancien associé de Moore, continue de
construire dans la Baie. Ses dernières

Wunsch, mit Hilfe von Lauben und Spalieren
eine Beziehung zwischen Bauwerk und Landschaft herzustellen, reinstes Kalifornien ist.
Maybeck entwarf auch eine Serie von Wohnhäusern, wobei anfangs Einflüsse der ein-
heimischen Bauwerken in der Bay Area
festzustellen sind: einfache Holzrahmen-
bauten mit Holzschindeln, die halbversteckt
unter den Bäumen stehen. Viel charakteri-
stischer freilich war die ehrgeizige Hearst Hall
(1899) mit ihren gotischen Bögen aus Holz-
laminat, den ersten ihrer Art. Hearst Hall,
1922 abgebrannt, findet einen Nachhall im
Jordan-Haus von ACE Architects, was nicht
ganz ohne Ironie ist – auf Schutt und Asche
eines Gebäudes erhebt sich die fast iden-
tische Kopie eines anderen, das lange vorher
ebenfalls den Flammen zum Opfer gefallen ist.

Während des Wiederaufbaus nach dem
großen Erdbeben von San Francisco von 1906
befaßte sich Maybeck mit feuer- und erd-
bebenfesten Techniken und Materialien.
Dabei verwendete er im Lawson-Haus in
Berkeley 1907 erstmals Beton.

Zur zweiten historischen Phase in der Bay
Area gehört die Arbeit von William Wurster
(1895–1973), der von den 20er Jahren bis
in die 60er tätig war. Sein Gregory Farmhouse
in Santa Cruz (1927), mit seinen niedrigen
Gebäuden im Ranch-Stil, die durch eine fort-
laufende Veranda verbunden werden und um
einen Innenhof angeordnet sind, wurde als
»Tischler-« oder »Slum-Stil« abgetan, obwohl
Wurster selbst darauf bestand, daß seine
Arbeit lediglich als Reaktion auf die Gegebenheiten zu verstehen sei. Man kann Parallelen

zwischen dem Gregory Farmhouse und dem
neuen Berggruen-Haus von Fernau und
Hartman ziehen, einer Ansammlung von
bäuerlich wirkenden Schuppen, die über ein
bewaldetes Grundstück verstreut sind, oder
dem Schnabel-Haus von Gehry in Los Angeles
(1989) mit seiner dorfähnlichen Volumen-
gruppierung. Zu den ungewöhnlichsten
Bauwerken Wursters zählt das Pope-Haus
Nr. 2 in Orinda (1940), das aus Blockbeton
und Wellblech gebaut ist und von einem
zentralen Innenhof beherrscht wird, der
beliebig durch große Schiebetüren um-
schlossen werden oder frei zugänglich sein
kann. Durch die Wahl der Materialien und den
einem Wellenkamm gleichenden »Schweif«
wird man an das McLane-Looke-Haus von
Saitowitz erinnert.

1

2

4

3

1–2 House + House Architecture's
Langmaid House presents itself
to the street as a grouping of
autonomous elements brought
together almost capriciously,
though the familiar materials and
language link it to other suburban
homes in the area.

3–4 House + House Architecture's
Hammonds House, on a
particularly steep and narrow
site, steps down the hillside from
the streetside garage.

1–2 De la rue, la Langmaid House
de House + House Architecture
semble être un groupement
d'éléments autonomes assemblés
presque capricieusement, bien
que les matériaux familiers et le
vocabulaire fassent le trait d'union
avec les autres maisons du quartier.

3–4 La Hammonds House de House
+ House Architecture, sur un site
étroit en pente très aiguë, descend
en escalier le long de la colline avec
pour point le plus haut son garage
sité au niveau de la rue.

1–2 Das Langmaid-Haus von House
+ House Architecture gibt sich
dem Betrachter als eine Gruppe
autonomer Elemente, durch ver-
traute Materialien und Ausdrucks-
form auf fast launische Weise mit
anderen Vorstadthäusern ver-
knüpft.

3–4 Das Hammonds-Haus von
House + House Architecture hat
eine besonders steile und enge
Hanglage. Die Garage liegt oben.

Wie schon Maybeck haben die Bay-Area-Architekten der zweiten Phase, wie Joseph Esherick, John Dinwiddie und John Funk, neue Technologien in einer für Nordkalifornien angemessen Weise erforscht. Bei Dinwiddies Roos-Haus in San Francisco (1938) und Funks Woerner-Haus in Marin County (1948) finden sich Verweise auf die Architektur von Le Corbusier bzw. Mies van der Rohe, aber die Ausführung erfolgte hier mit den in der Bay Area gängigen Materialien. Der Stil ihrer Arbeiten läßt sich vielleicht am besten als »regionaler Modernismus« bezeichnen.

Die in den 60er Jahren entstandene Arbeit von Charles Moore, der in Partnerschaft mit Lyndon Turnbull Whitaker tätig war, gehört zur dritten Phase der Architekturtradition in der Bay Area. Bei Projekten wie der Sea

Ranch, nördlich von San Francisco, ließ sich Moore von der ländlichen Schlichtheit der herkömmlichen kalifornischen Holzscheune und von der spartanischen Strenge inspirieren, die er in der Arbeit von Louis Kahn entdeckt hatte. Der frühere Partner Moores, William Turnbull, ist noch immer im Raum San Francisco tätig: bei den Foothill-Studentenwohnheimen, die er vor kurzem in Berkeley baute, verwendete er ländliche Formen sowie strukturelle Elemente und Verkleidungen aus Holz; auffällig ist auch ein ausgefallener Sinn für Proportionen, ähnlich dem von Moore.

Die Geschichte der vierten Phase der Bay-Area-Tradition ist noch noch geschrieben, obwohl sich ein Aspekt bereits abzeichnet: Sie läßt sich weniger klar definieren als die früheren Phasen. Der ästhetischen Kollision

zwischen den neuen Häuser von Moore Ruble Yudell, Saitowitz, Frank Israel und James Gillam an der Ecke von Alvarado und Vicente in der Brandzone nach zu urteilen, läßt sich vielleicht nur ein einziges typisches Element herauskristallisieren, nämlich ein Gefühl für die Lage. Wegen des Brandes brauchen die mit dem Bau neuer Häuser in diesen Bergen beauftragten Architekten bei ihren Entwürfen keine Rücksicht auf benachbarte Gebäude, auf Bäume oder andere Vegetation zu nehmen; die üblichen Grenzen des geistigen Freiraums sind, wenn man von den strengen Bauvorschriften einmal absieht, hier für sie kein Hindernis. Die Häuser, die früher hier standen, mußten sich in eine bereits existierende, architektonisch und gartenbaulich gestaltete Landschaft einfügen; für

5

6

5–6 Siegal & Strain's Wayne Dinkelspiel House is entered through a pergola and intimate garden that link it to the landscape.

5–6 On pénètre dans la Wayne Dinkelspiel House de Siegal & Strain par une pergola et un jardin intime qui met en relation la maison et le paysage.

5–6 Das Wayne-Dinkelspiel-Haus von Siegal & Strain betritt man durch eine Pergola und einen stillen Garten, der das Objekt in die Natur einbindet.

réalisations incluent la résidence pour étudiants à Berkeley (Foothill Student Housing) où il emploie des formes traditionnelles à la région, des éléments de structure et de revêtement en bois, et où il fait preuve d'un sens étrange des proportions, semblable à celui de Moore.

L'histoire de la quatrième période de la tradition de la Baie reste à écrire. Elle semble cependant plus complexe à définir que les périodes précédentes. Les maisons récemment réalisées par Moore Ruble Yudell, Saitowitz, Frank Israel et James Gillam, à l'angle de Alvarado et de Vicente dans la zone de l'incendie, manquent certes d'harmonie les unes par rapport aux autres, mais on ne peut reprocher aux architectes d'avoir su prendre le site en considération. Grâce à

l'incendie, les architectes qui construisent sur les Hills peuvent concevoir sans avoir à prendre en compte les maisons voisines, les arbres ou la végétation, ni les contraintes habituelles, si ce n'est les exigences imposées par le code de la construction et de l'habitation. Les maisons que ces architectes remplacent devaient s'intégrer au paysage architectural et au paysage planté. Les nouvelles maisons en sont dépourvues et n'en possède aujourd'hui que le souvenir. Ce qu'elles offrent, en revanche, c'est un site vierge, un lieu extraordinaire et la possibilité d'élaborer un programme en proche collaboration avec le maître d'ouvrage.

Chacune des maisons présentées dans ce livre exprime le souci de concevoir des espaces maîtrisés dans lesquels le

programme d'habitation se lit avec clarté. Contrairement à la plupart des nouvelles maisons des Hills, ces constructions emploient un vocabulaire subtil comprenant des écrans, des matériaux et des structures miroirs qui rompent les volumes. Ce sont aussi des conceptions osées, car on distingue leur originalité même de loin. Cependant leur aspect est résolu et simple, une simplicité issue de la grande tradition moderne – aussi importante que la tradition colonialiste espagnole ou que l'éclectisme mi-Tudor mi-élisabéthain. Alors que la plupart des maisons des Hills se contentent de reproduire un vocabulaire passéiste sans originalité, ces projets assurent la continuité des principes modernes et offrent une architecture adaptée à la vie de la Côte Ouest en cette fin de siècle.

die neuen Wohnhäuser existiert eine solche Landschaft nicht oder nur in der Erinnerung. Was die Architekten hier vorfinden, ist ein leeres Grundstück, eine herrliche Lage und die Gelegenheit, in enger Zusammenarbeit mit den Kunden ein Programm zu entwickeln.

Gemeinsam ist allen in diesem Buch dargestellten Häusern das Bemühen um die Schaffung kontrollierter Räume, in denen ein Wohnprogramm mit größter Klarheit zum Ausdruck kommt. Im Gegensatz zu vielen Neubauten in diese Gegend bedienen sich diese Gebäude einer eher subtilen Sprache; ihre Masse wird durch den Einsatz von Sichtblenden und spiegelnden Materialien, aber auch auf strukturellem Weg aufgelockert. Diese Häuser haben etwas Gewagtes: Selbst aus der Entfernung gesehen, behaupten sie

ihre Individualität. Dennoch sind sie auch zweckdienlich und einfach, mit einer Schlichtheit, die aus der großen Tradition des Modernismus rührt, die ebenso einen Anspruch auf Echtheit hat wie die Traditionen des spanischen Kolonialstils oder des tudorbethanischen Eklektizismus. Während sich sehr viele Neubauten in den Hills darauf beschränken, ein Vokabular aus der Vergangenheit ohne jegliche Originalität nachzuplappern, erweitern diese Bauwerke die Prinzipien des Modernismus und schaffen eine Architektur, die dem Leben an der US-Westküste im ausklingenden 20. Jahrhundert angemessen ist.

McLane-Looke House

Stanley Saitowitz

The form of the McLane-Looke House is determined by its site. The plan is derived from the non-orthogonal shape of the plot; the section reflects the contours of the hillside. Both factors are followed to a startling extent, resulting in a building that is delicate without being weak.

The approach to the house is dominated by the rolling curve of the roof, which projects over the front façade, announcing the entrance and sheltering the south-facing garden from the street. The shape of this roof mirrors the crest of the hill on which the house stands; its absolute specificity to its site expresses the seriousness with which Saitowitz has applied his concept of geological architecture – 'the continuation of the geographic evolution of a site through building; the turning [of] a site into a state of mind' – to generate form.

The main feature of the garden is an outcrop of rock. The screen wall facing this is made of taut, industrial materials – glass and corrugated aluminium set in a checkerboard pattern – echoing the texture of the rocks and dividing and reflecting both house and garden. The changing fall of light animates the wall, qualifying the static materiality of the building. This hard and nervy wall ends at a shockingly sharp point, the junction with an almost windowless curved stucco wall, like a soft bag at the back of the lot.

Behind the glass and aluminium screen between garden and shelter, a curved wall continues the rockscape into the house, setting up the geometry of the interior. This wall, which supports a gallery above, contains the programme elements of fireplace, kitchen and storage, and leads to the stair. As a wall of services, it divides the main level into living, dining, cooking and family spaces. On the west, facing the Golden Gate, the house is sliced to give a triangular court outside the dining room, looking through the corner of the property to sundown.

The presence of the rock outcrop is felt throughout the house. Saitowitz explains the geometry of the interior as a reaction to and a reflection of the rock. Certainly it is hard to imagine the division of space on the bedroom floor as having been generated by anything as mundane as function.

The texture of the interior contrasts dramatically with the industrial materials of the exterior: it is highly finished and finely detailed, though some elements of structure – steel-bar joists, for instance – are left exposed.

1 The form of the roof follows the ground's contours.
2–3 The front façade leans over the deep carport. Over the carport are a bedroom, studio and bathroom.

1 La forme du toit suit les contours du terrain.
2–3 La façade frontale dépasse au-dessus du profond garage ouvert. Une chambre, un atelier et une salle de bains sont disposés au-dessus du auvent.

1 Das Dach folgt den Boden-konturen.
2–3 Die Frontfassade lehnt sich über den langen Einstellplatz. Darüber liegen ein Schlafzimmer, Studio und Badezimmer.

1

Bestimmend für die Form des McLane-Looke-Hauses ist seine Lage. Der Grundriß erklärt sich aus der Unregelmäßigkeit des Grundstücks; der Querschnitt orientiert sich an den Konturen des Abhangs. Beide Faktoren kommen in geradezu erstaunlichem Ausmaß zum Tragen, und das Ergebnis ist ein Gebäude, das zerbrechlich wirkt, ohne schwach zu sein.

Die Zufahrt zum Haus wird von der Kurve des Daches beherrscht, das über die vordere Fassade hinausragt, den Eingang markiert und den nach Süden liegenden Garten von der Straße abschirmt. Das Dach hat die gleiche Form wie die Spitze des Berges, auf dem das Haus steht; daß die Form mit Bezug auf den Standort absolut spezifisch ist, beweist die Ernsthaftig-keit, mit der Saitowitz sein Konzept von der geologischen Architektur zur Anwendung gebracht hat – »die Weiterführung der geographischen Evolution eines Standorts durch den Bau; die Verwandlung eines Standorts in einen Geisteszustand« –, um Form hervorzubringen.

Das Auffälligste am Garten ist eine herausragende Felsnase. Die ihr gegenüberliegende Außenwand besteht aus straffen Industriematerialien – Glas und Aluminiumwellblech in einem Schachbrettmuster. Sie greifen die Oberflächenstruktur der Felsen wieder auf, Haus und Garten werden voneinander getrennt und zugleich reflektiert. Durch den wechselnden Licht-einfall wird die Wand belebt, die statische Stofflichkeit des Gebäudes gemildert.

Diese harte, dreiste Außenwand endet in einer spitzen Ecke, wo sich eine nahezu fensterlose, gebogene Stuckmauer an-schließt, die wie ein weicher Sack wirkend das Grundstück nach hinten abgrenzt.

Hinter der Glas- und Aluminiumwand zwischen Garten und Unterkunft wird die Felsenlandschaft durch eine geschwungene Mauer in das Haus hineingetragen und legt somit die Geometrie des Innenraums fest. Diese Mauer, die eine darüberliegende Galerie trägt, enthält die Programmelemente Kamin, Küche und Stauraum und führt zur Treppe. Als Trennwand unterteilt sie die Hauptetage in Wohn-, Eß-, Koch-, und Familienräume. Im Westen, zur Golden-Gate-Brücke hin, ist das Haus der Länge nach aufgeschnitten; dadurch ent-

2

C'est le relief du site qui a déterminé la forme de la McLane-Looke House. Le plan est issu de la configuration non orthogonale du terrain et la coupe reflète les contours du flan de la colline. Ces deux éléments ont été poussés au plus haut degré et le résultat est une construction légère sans pour autant être fragile.

L'accès à la maison est caractérisé par la courbe ondulée du toit qui dépasse de la façade avant, marque l'entrée et protège de la rue le jardin orienté vers le sud. La forme du toit reflète la crête de la colline sur laquelle se trouve la maison. Sa remarquable adéquation au site démontre avec quel sérieux Saitowitz a mis en pratique son concept d'architecture géologique qu'il définit comme «la

continuation de l'évolution géographique d'un site par une construction, la transformation d'un site en un état d'esprit» pour générer une forme.

La caractéristique principale du jardin est l'affleurement du rocher. Le mur écran qui lui fait face est conçu avec des matériaux industriels en tension (verre et aluminium ondulé alternés comme sur un échiquier) qui rappellent la texture des pierres, divise et réfléchit tant le jardin que la maison. A la tombée de la nuit, la lumière anime le mur, dissipant ainsi la matérialité statique de la maison. Ce mur dur et fibreux se prolonge jusqu'au point de jonction avec un mur en stuc sans ouvertures, ou presque, qui ressemble à une masse souple au fond du terrain.

Derrière l'écran de verre et d'aluminium qui sépare le jardin de l'abri, un mur en courbe poursuit la ligne du rocher dans la maison, dessinant la géométrie de l'intérieur. Il a aussi pour rôle de soutenir la galerie de l'étage supérieur, de renfermer les éléments de programme (la cheminée, de la cuisine et des rangements) et de mener à l'escalier. En tant que vide technique, ce mur divise le niveau principal en espaces salon, repas, cuisine et familial. Côté sud, face au Golden Gate, la maison est tranchée de façon à former une cour triangulaire devant la salle à manger qui est orientée vers l'angle de la propriété, face au soleil couchant.

L'affleurement du rocher dégage une présence qui se ressent à travers la maison

entière. Pour Saitowitz, la géométrie de l'intérieur est à la fois une réaction à cette présence et le reflet de ce rocher. Il est bien difficile d'imaginer que la distribution de l'espace à l'étage des chambres a été organisée en fonction des attributs ordinaires du fonctionnel.

La texture de l'intérieur et les matériaux industriels de l'extérieur offrent un contraste saisissant. Les finitions sont parfaites et les détails parachevés tandis que d'autres éléments de la structure comme par exemple les solives en acier des gîtes sont laissés nus.

steht ein dreieckiger Innenhof vor dem Eßzimmer, mit Blick über die Ecke des Grundstücks auf die untergehende Sonne.

Die Gegenwart der Felsnase ist überall im Haus zu spüren. Saitowitz erklärt die Geometrie des Interieurs als Reaktion auf den Felsen und zugleich als seine Reflektion. Man kann sich jedenfalls nur schwer vorstellen, daß die Raumeinteilung auf der Schlafzimmeretage von etwas so Banalem wie der Funktion bestimmt worden sein könnte.

Die Oberflächenstruktur im Inneren steht in krassem Gegensatz zu den Industriematerialien, die für die Außenseite verwendet wurden: Sie ist hoch verarbeitet, obwohl einige Strukturelemente – wie zum Beispiel die Stahlunterzüge – freiliegen.

3

1–3 A projecting curve of the roof protects the entrance to the house, and shelters the south-facing garden.
4–5 The startlingly sharp junction of the house's long sides, where aluminium meets stucco, is emphasised by the curve of the balcony.

1–3 Une courbe saillante du toit protège l'entrée de la maison et abrite le jardin orienté vers le sud.
4–5 La jonction extrêmement aiguë des côtés de la maison, à l'endroit où l'aluminium rencontre le stuc, est accentuée par la courbe du balcon.

1–3 Ein gebogener Dachvorsprung schützt den Hauseingang und den nach Süden weisenden Garten.
4–5 Die schockierend spitze Ecke der langen Seiten, in der Aluminium auf Stuck trifft, wird durch den Balkonbogen akzentuiert.

4

5

1

2

3

1–4 Corrugated-aluminium panels make a richly patterned composition, constantly changing in the sun and dramatically lit at night.

1–4 Les panneaux d'aluminium ondulés, qui créent une composition au motif riche, ne cessent de changer selon le soleil et sont inondés de lumière la nuit.

1–4 Wellbleche aus Aluminium setzen sich zu einer stark gemusterten Komposition zusammen, die im Sonnenlicht ständig ihr Aussehen verändert und nachts dramatisch beleuchtet wird.

4

1

2

3

4

1–3 The double-height living space
has openings at both levels framing
the garden and the sky.
4–5 A curving wall establishes the
geometry of the interior,
supporting the gallery and
containing a number of elements –
fireplace, kitchen and storage.

1–3 Le salon d'une double hauteur
possède des ouvertures, à chacun
des niveaux, qui encadrent le
jardin et le ciel.
4–5 Le mur en courbe définit la
géométrie de l'intérieur, porte la
galerie et contient des éléments tels
que la cheminée, la cuisine et les
rangements.

1–3 Der Wohnraum in doppelter Höhe
weist auf beiden Ebenen Öff-
nungen auf, die den Blick auf Garten und Himmel rahmen.
4–5 Eine geschwungene Mauer legt
die Geometrie des Innenraums
fest, trägt die Galerie und enthält
die Elemente Kamin, Küche und
Stauraum.

5

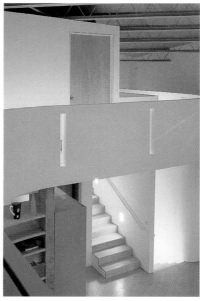

1–4 The gallery leads to the master suite, beyond which a deck extends around the tip of the house, providing a view back to the rocks in the garden.

1–4 La galerie mène à l'appartement derrière lequel une plate-forme s'étend le long de l'extrémité de la maison offrant une vue aux rochers du jardin lorsqu'on se retourne.

1–4 Die Galerie führt zum Wohnbereich, hinter dem eine Terrasse an der Spitze des Hauses wieder den Blick auf die Felsen im Garten freigibt.

4

1 Half a level above the ground floor, the studio leans out over the carport.
2 The roof is simply supported on exposed steel-bar joists.
3 The kitchen, contained within the curved wall. Here the floor finish changes from maple to terrazzo; cabinets are maple.
4 Simple finishes characterise the interior, contrasting with the industrial materials of the main façade.
5 An artful elision of exterior and interior created with aluminium and glass.

1 Un demi-étage au-dessus du sol, l'atelier dépasse au-dessus du garage ouvert.
2 Le toit est porté par des poutres de solives en acier exposées.
3 La cuisine, à l'intérieur du mur en courbe. Ici, les matériaux du sol vont de l'érable au granito. Les armoires sont en érable.
4 Les finitions simples caractérisent l'intérieur et contrastent avec les matériaux industriels utilisés pour la façade principale.
5 Une élision ingénieuse de l'extérieur et de l'intérieur grâce à l'emploi de verre et d'aluminium.

1 Auf halber Ebene über dem Erdgeschoß ragt das Studio über den Einstellplatz vor.
2 Das Dach wird einfach von freiliegenden Stahlunterzügen getragen.
3 Die in der geschwungenen Wand untergebrachte Küche. Hier geht der Fußboden von Ahorn in Terrazzo über; die Schränke sind in Ahorn gehalten.
4 Schlichte Oberflächen kennzeichnen das Interieur, in krassem Gegensatz zu den Industriematerialien an der Hauptfassade.
5 Eine gelungene Elision von Interieur und Exterieur, geschaffen aus Aluminium und Glas.

4

5

Top floor plan

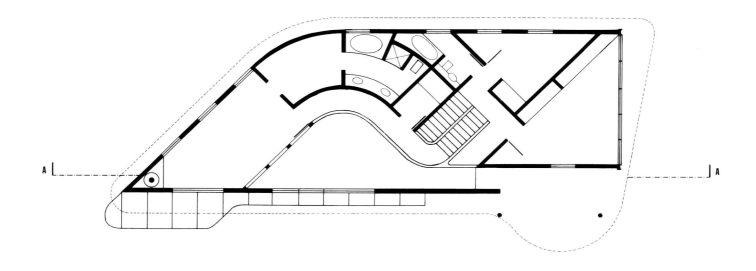

Ground floor plan

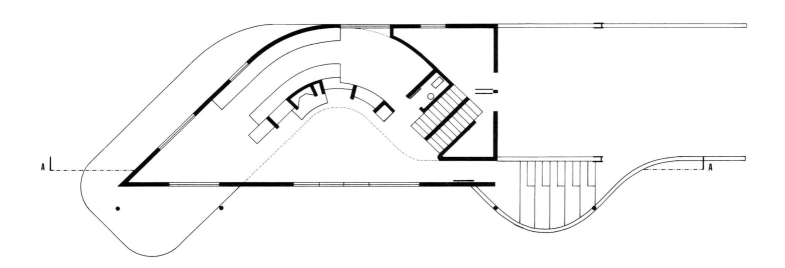

Stanley Saitowitz
1992

Address 6131 Ocean View, Oakland CA
Design Stanley Saitowitz
Project architect John Winder
Project team Ulysses Lim, Daniel Luis
General contractor Natoma Construction
Size house 2400 square feet;
carport 440 square feet
Cost US$450,000
Publications *Elle Decor* (2/96); Stanley
Saitowitz, *Stanley Saitowitz:
Architecture at Rice 33*, Princeton
Architectural Press 1996

section A–A

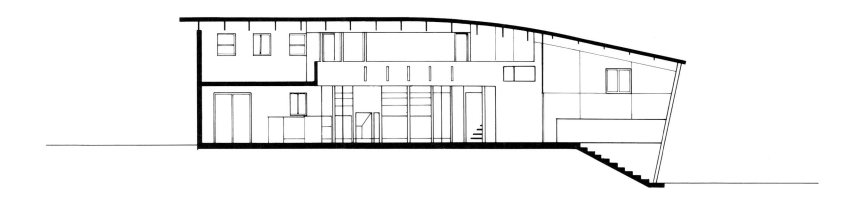

Site plan

Becker House

Jim Jennings
Arkhitekture

Like Philip Banta's xyz House, the Becker House occupies a steeply sloping site. It is divided functionally into two volumes: the larger one houses the living spaces for the clients, while the smaller second box contains practical spaces such as a studio and garage as well as rooms for two university-aged children. The volumes are differentiated externally by the use of cladding: cement board for the larger one and corrugated metal for the smaller one. They are linked by a sheet of etched green glass on the street front and on the canyon side by an open deck, extended by broad stairs to a platform with breathtaking views.

The front door opens straight into the kitchen, which is very unkitchenlike.

Windows above cupboards and alcoves are glazed with opaque glass, leading the eye up, away from the fittings. The materials used for services – black wood and marble – obscure their function. The corresponding space in the metal-clad wing has horizontal strips of clear glazing, not framing views but letting in lines of sky, windows on to the weather.

Every aspect of the structure has been stripped to its essence. Look, for instance, at the way guttering is avoided: in order to maintain the purity of the form and do away with ugly pipework, considerable thought has gone into the detailing of the water channels off the roof. Forget form following function – this is an ethereal architecture, refined to the maximum.

1–3 Built on a steeply sloping site, the Becker House is essentially two simple boxes.

1–3 Construite sur un site en pente aiguë, la Becker House consiste en deux volumes simples.

1–3 Das an einem steilen Hang liegende Becker-Haus besteht im Prinzip aus zwei einfachen Kästen.

1

2

Wie das xyz-Haus von Banta steht das Becker-Haus auf einem Grundstück mit starkem Gefälle. Es ist von der Funktion her in zwei Abschnitte unterteilt: Im größeren sind die Wohnräume der Bauherren untergebracht, im zweiten, kleineren Kasten befinden sich neben zweckgebundenen Räumen, wie einem Studio und einer Garage, auch die Zimmer von zwei Kindern im Studentenalter. Äußerlich werden die beiden Abschnitte durch die Verwendung unterschiedlichen Verkleidungsmaterials differenziert: Betonplatten für das größere, Wellblech für das kleinere. An der Seite zur Straße hin werden sie durch grünes Ätzglas, auf der zum Canyon hin durch eine offene Terrasse miteinander verbunden, von der eine breite Treppe zu

einer Plattform mit atemberaubender Aussicht führt.

Durch die Haustür kommt man direkt in die Küche, die überhaupt nicht küchenartig wirkt. Die Fenster über den Schränken und Alkoven sind aus Milchglas; sie lenken den Blick nach oben, fort von der Einrichtung. Das Material für die Arbeitsflächen (schwarzes Holz und Marmor) kaschiert deren Funktion. Der entsprechende Raum im metallverkleideten Flügel weist horizontale Streifen aus klarem Fensterglas auf, die weniger dazu dienen, die Aussicht einzurahmen, als vielmehr den Blick auf Himmelsstreifen freigeben – Wetterfenster.

Jeder Aspekt der Struktur wurde auf das Wesentliche reduziert. Man nehme als

Beispiel nur den Verzicht auf Regenrinnen: Um die Reinheit der Form zu bewahren und häßliche Röhren zu vermeiden, hat man sich über den Ablauf des Wassers vom Dach viele Gedanken gemacht. Daß die Form sich nach der Funktion richten sollte, kann man ignorieren – hier handelt es sich um eine ätherische Architektur, in höchstem Grade kultiviert.

Comme la xyz House de Banta, la Becker House est construite sur un site en pente aiguë. Les fonctions sont divisées en deux volumes : le plus grand contient les espaces de vie du maître d'ouvrage, l'autre, plus petit, renferme le studio, le garage et les chambres des enfants âgés d'une vingtaine d'années. Vus de l'extérieur, les deux volumes se distinguent par leur revêtement – panneaux de ciment pour le plus grand et métal ondulé pour le plus petit. Ces deux éléments sont reliés, côté rue, par une feuille de verre vert gravé à l'eau forte et, côté canyon, par le plancher d'une terrasse ouverte, prolongée par de grandes marches qui permettent l'accès à une plate-forme d'où la vue est à couper le souffle.

La porte d'entrée ouvre directement sur la cuisine, qui, d'ailleurs, ne ressemble à une cuisine que de très loin. Les fenêtres, au-dessus des placards, ainsi que les niches sont en verre opaque et attirent le regard vers le haut faisant ainsi oublier la présence des installations encastrées. Les équipements sont en des matériaux tels que le bois noir et le marbre, qui masquent leurs fonctions. La pièce correspondante, située dans l'aile habillée de métal, est agrémentée de bandes horizontales en verre transparent qui n'encadrent pas la vue mais laissent pénétrer dans la pièce des lignes du ciel qui sont des fenêtres sur le temps qu'il fait dehors.

Chaque aspect de la structure a été mis à nu pour en faire ressortir l'essence. Regardez, par exemple, comme on a su éviter l'installation d'une gouttière : afin de conserver la pureté de la forme et de supprimer toute tuyauterie hideuse, les conduits d'eau qui descendent du toit ont été étudiés dans les moindres détails. Oubliez le principe qui dicte que la forme suit la fonction. Il s'agit, ici, d'une architecture éthérée, des plus raffinées.

3

1 Narrow strip windows – clear
glass in the metal-clad wing – are
designed to control views of the
sky, providing dramatic changes
of light within the house.
2 One box is clad in cement board,
the other in aluminium panels.

1 Les fenêtres étroites en bande
– verre transparent dans l'aile
revêtue de métal – sont conçues
pour encadrer la vue sur le ciel et
offrir de magnifiques changements
de lumière à la maison.
2 Un des volumes est revêtu de
panneaux de ciment, l'autre de
panneaux d'aluminium.

1 Schmale Fenster – im metallverkleideten Flügel aus klarem
Glas – geben den kontrollierten
Blick auf Himmelsstreifen frei
und sorgen für dramatische Licht-
wechsel im Haus.
2 Ein Kasten ist mit Betonplatten
verkleidet, der andere mit Alu-
miniumblechen.

3

3 The two wings of the house are joined by an etched green glass screen. The division of the house is most clearly seen from here.

4 Cement board detailed with precision; not even down pipes are allowed to compromise the simplicity.

3 Les deux ailes de la maison sont reliées par un écran en verre vert gravé à l'eau forte. On distingue parfaitement la division de la maison à cet endroit.

4 Panneaux de ciment détaillés avec une grande précision. Même les conduits d'eaux qui habituellement descendent du toit ne sont pas autorisés au risque de compromettre la simplicité du design.

3 Die beiden Flügel werden durch eine Sichtblende aus grünem Ätzglas miteinander verbunden. Von hier aus sieht man die Teilung des Hauses am deutlichsten.

4 Präzise ausgearbeitete Betonplatten; nicht einmal die Fallrohre dürfen die Schlichtheit kompromittieren.

4

1–3 A large deck, crossed by a bridge, is sheltered from the wind.
4 The most dramatic element of the house, the platform protruding from between the wings, appears to jut out into space.

1–3 La grande plate-forme, traversée par un pont, est à l'abri du vent.
4 L'attribut le plus frappant de la maison est la plate-forme qui dépasse des deux ailes et s'avance dans l'espace.

1–3 Eine große, von einer Brücke überquerte Terrasse, liegt windgeschützt.
4 Das dramatischste Element des Hauses: Die Plattform zwischen den Flügeln scheint frei in den Raum hinauszuragen.

4

1–2 Taking advantage of the slope, the house is entered from the top floor.
3–5 An etched glass screen protecting the stairs exemplifies the quality of the internal detailing.

1–2 Grâce à la pente, on entre dans la maison par le dernier étage.
3–5 Un écran en verre gravé à l'eau forte protège l'escalier et met en valeur la qualité des détails intérieurs.

1–2 Unter Nutzung der Hanglage führt der Hauseingang in das Obergeschoß.
3–5 Die Ätzglasscheibe zum Schutz der Treppe verdeutlicht die Detailqualität des Interieurs.

1–2 The lower floor is open to the
landscape, detailed with precision,
and flooded with light.
3–4 Dining and kitchen areas on the
top floor of the metal-clad wing.
Materials in the kitchen are black
marble and dark wood. Views
from here are of the sky.
5 A shower with a view.

1–2 L'étage inférieur, qui est inondé
de lumière et donne sur le paysage,
est détaillé avec précision.
3–4 Les espaces salon et cuisine du
dernier étage de l'aile revêtue de
métal. Les matériaux de la cuisine
sont en marbre et bois noir. D'ici,
on voit le ciel.
5 Une douche avec vue.

1–2 Das Untergeschoß öffnet sich zur
Landschaft; präzise ausgearbeitet
und lichtüberflutet.
3–4 Eßzimmer und Küche im Obergeschoß des metallverkleideten
Flügels. Die Küche präsentiert sich
in schwarzem Marmor und dunk-
lem Holz. Von hier aus sieht man
den Himmel.
5 Dusche mit Aussicht.

3

4

5

Top floor plan

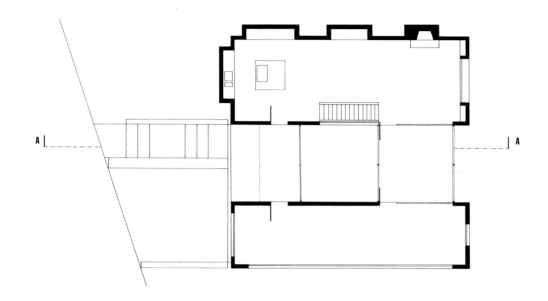

Lower floor plan

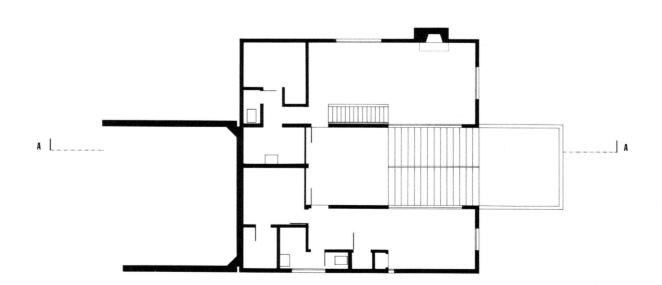

Becker House
Jim Jennings Arkhitekture
1994
Address 340 Lombard Street, San Francisco
CA
Client Steven and Nancy Oliver
Design team Jim Jennings, Tim Perks
Construction administration Cheri Fraser
General contractor Oliver & Company
Structural consultant Sear-Brown Group (Kevin Clinch)
Size house 4500 square feet; garage
1600 square feet; terraces 1125
square feet; apartment 924 square
feet
Exhibited San Francisco Museum of Modern
Art 1991, drawings and model in
permanent collection

section A–A

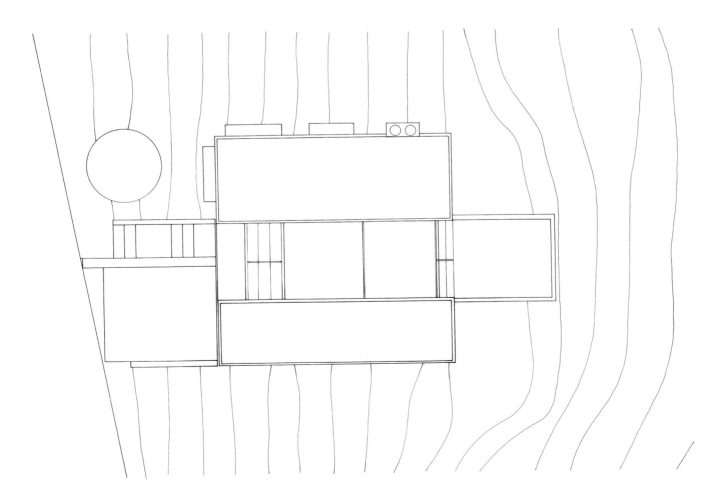

Site plan

XYZ House

Philip Banta &
Associates Architecture

The site is difficult – a narrow lot on a steep slope. The building envelope is further restricted by fire-code and sprinkler regulations. The architect's response is a 'vertical working volume' – a stack of rigorously Cartesian spaces qualified by two curving balconies and a podlike enclosure on two floors that pops out of one wall, with brutal earthquake bracing strapped on to the façade.

The clients, collectors of American art and furniture of the 1940s, 1950s and 1960s, wanted a modernist house protected at the street side but open to the outdoors. These requirements are met by a simple strategy: a four-storey glazed box, a 'vertical gallery' for the owners' art collection, is cradled between deep stucco walls which provide physical and visual protection. In the centre of these volumes, a curved aluminium enclosure contains all the rooms using water: kitchen, bathrooms and laundry. Curvilinear decks raised on seismic steel struts create a walkway circuit to the outdoors and with the concrete interior floors become part of the living-room hearth, kitchen and door thresholds. In plan the house appears remarkably lucid; in section it is absolutely rigid.

The geometry of boxes allows for a free-flowing plan at the heart of the house. The essentially divisionless space of the main living level provides unlimited circular movement, in contrast to the confinement usually imposed by vertical solutions. The decks and broad roof overhangs offer sunshading; the concrete provides thermal mass for passive solar heating; the double-height living room and stair tower offer natural ventilation potential for the whole house.

1–2 Architectural experimentation: the rectangles of modernism overlaid with organic shapes and bolt-on earthquake bracing.
3 A house for collectors.

1–2 Expérience architecturale : Les rectangles modernistes sont superposés aux formes organiques et aux contreventements boulonnés qui protègent la structure en cas de secousses sismiques.
3 Une maison pour collectionneur.

1–2 Architektonische Experimente: Die Rechtecke des Modernismus werden von organischen Formen und verankerten Erdbebenstreben überlagert.
3 Ein Haus für Sammler.

3

Le terrain est difficile : une parcelle étroite en pente aiguë. L'enveloppe de la maison est conforme aux exigences de sécurité contre l'incendie et de la réglementation en matière d'extincteurs de feu. La solution de l'architecte est donc un volume en mouvement vertical – un enchaînement d'espaces superposés très cartésiens ponctué par deux balcons et un espace fermé oval, sur deux niveaux, qui dépasse de l'un des murs. La façade est équipée d'un système de contreventement imposant visant à protéger la structure en cas de secousses sismiques.

Le maître d'ouvrage, un collectionneur de meubles et d'art américain des années 40, 50 et 60, voulait une maison de style moderne à la fois protégée de la rue et ouverte sur l'extérieur. La stratégie employée pour répondre à ses demandes est simple : il s'agit d'une boîte en verre de quatre étages, qui constitue une «galerie verticale» pour la collection, logée entre deux murs profonds en stuc qui offrent une protection physique et visuelle. Au centre de ces volumes, un espace courbe en aluminium renferme toutes les pièces d'eau : la cuisine, les salles de bains et la blanchisserie. Les platelages curvilignes en béton, tenus sur des jambes de force antisismiques en acier, dessinent un parcours menant aux accès vers l'extérieur et, grâce aux planchers intérieurs en béton, s'intègrent au foyer du salon, à la cuisine et aux seuils de porte. En plan, la maison est remarquablement claire. En coupe, elle est extrêmement cartésienne.

La disposition géométrique des boîtes permet d'avoir au centre de la maison un plan flexible. Les espaces sans cloison du niveau principal permettent un mouvement libre sans aucune restriction, bien différents des pièces fermées qu'imposent souvent les solutions verticales. Les platelages et le large toit en surplomb offrent de l'ombre. Le béton agit comme une masse thermique, génératrice de chaleur solaire passive. Le salon, d'une double hauteur de plafond, et la cage d'escalier sont une source potentielle de ventilation naturelle pour l'ensemble de la maison.

Die Lage ist problematisch – ein schmales Grundstück an einem steilen Hang. Feuer- und Sprinklervorschriften schränken den Freiraum weiter ein. Der Architekt reagierte, indem er ein »vertikales Arbeitsvolumen« schuf – einen Stoß von rigoros kartesischen Räumen, aufgelockert durch zwei geschwungene Balkone und eine schotenähnliche Kapsel, die auf zwei Etagen aus der Wand ragt, wobei gewaltige Streben für den Fall eines Erdbebens an der Fassade verankert sind.

Die Bauherren, die amerikanische Kunst und Möbel aus den 40er, 50er und 60er Jahren sammeln, wünschten sich ein modernistisches Haus, das zur Straßenseite hin geschützt, der Außenwelt gegenüber jedoch aufgeschlossen sein sollte. Diese Anforderungen wurden auf einfache Weise erfüllt: Ein vierstöckiger verglaster Kasten, eine »vertikale Galerie«, die die Kunstsammlung der Besitzer aufnehmen soll, nistet zwischen dicken Stuckmauern, die Schutz bieten, auch vor unerwünschten Blicken. Im Mittelpunkt dieser Raumkörper liegt eine gebogene Aluminiumzelle, in der der sich alle Räume mit Wasserbedarf befinden: Küche, Badezimmer und Waschküche. Auf seismischen Stahlstreben ruhende, geschwungene Terrassen schaffen eine runde Bahn als Verbindung mit der Außenwelt; zusammen mit den Betonfußböden im Inneren sind sie Teil des offenen Kamins im Wohnzimmer, der Küche und der Türschwellen. Im Grundriß wirkt das Haus bemerkenswert transparent; im Querschnitt ist es absolut starr.

Die Kastengeometrie gestattet eine freizügige Grundrißgestaltung im Kern des Hauses. Auf der Hauptwohnebene wird der Raum im Prinzip gar nicht unterteilt, so daß eine unbegrenzte, kreisförmige Bewegung möglich ist – ganz im Gegensatz zu den sonst im allgemeinen bei vertikalen Lösungen existierenden Beschränkungen. Die Terrassen und die breiten Dachvorsprünge bieten Schutz vor der Sonne; der Beton liefert die nötige thermische Masse für eine passive Solarheizung; die doppelte Höhe des Wohnzimmers und der Treppenturm ermöglichen eine natürliche Belüftung des gesamten Hauses.

1

1–2 The XYZ House rears up, its geometry and verticality performing an uncompromising balancing act on the difficult site. The balconies and the overhanging roof shade the glazed wall.
3–6 Simple forms detailed to express strength.
7 The 'x' of the earthquake-bracing structure.

1–2 La XYZ House s'élève tandis que sa géométrie et sa verticalité mettent en scène un numéro d'équilibriste délicat sur un site difficile. Les balcons et le toit en surplomb offrent de l'ombre au mur en verre.
3–6 Formes simples et détaillées expriment la force du bâtiment.
7 Le «x» de la structure des contreventements contre les secousses sismiques.

1–2 Das XYZ-Haus erhebt sich – Geometrie und Vertikalität in einem kompromißlosen Balanceakt auf schwierigem Gelände. Die Balkone und das hervorstehende Dach werfen Schatten auf die glasierte Mauer.
3–6 Schlichte Formen offenbaren im Detail Stärke.
7 Das Kreuz der seismischen Struktur.

2

3

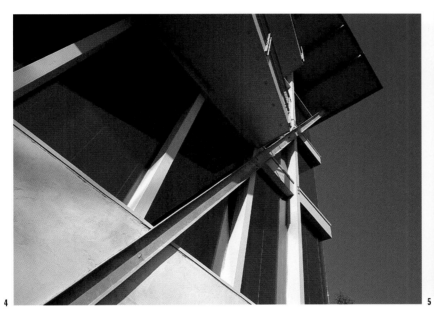

4

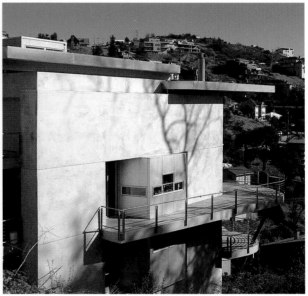

5

6

7

1–3 The double-height living room and stair tower provide natural ventilation for the whole house.
4 The curved aluminium 'pod' contains all the rooms where water is needed – kitchen, bathrooms and laundry.

1–3 Le salon d'une double hauteur et la cage d'escalier sont une source potentielle de ventilation naturelle pour l'ensemble de la maison.
4 Un espace courbe en aluminium renferme toutes les pièces d'eau – la cuisine, les salles de bains et la blanchisserie.

1–3 Das Wohnzimmer in doppelter Höhe und der Treppenturm sorgen für eine natürliche Belüftung des ganzen Hauses.
4 Die gebogene Aluminiumzelle enthält alle Räume mit Wasserbedarf: Küche, Badezimmer und Waschküche.

4

1–5 Internally, the house is planned as a vertical gallery for displaying the owners' collections of art and furniture.
6–7 Although the house is four storeys high, the problems of too much verticality have been alleviated by the undivided main living space.

1–5 La conception de l'intérieur de la maison est une «galerie verticale» destinée à exposer la collection de meubles et de peintures du propriétaire.
6–7 Bien que la maison soit d'une hauteur de quatre étages, les problèmes de verticalité sont résolus par l'indivision de l'espace principal.

1–5 Innen ist das Haus als vertikale Galerie für die Kunst- und Möbelsammlung des Bauherren ausgelegt.
6–7 Obwohl das Haus vier Geschosse hat, wurde das Problem der starken Vertikalen durch den offenen Plan des Hauptwohnraums bewältigt.

1 A place to paint.
2 Between the house and hill, a protected and private space is a bonus of the house's geometry.
3–5 The precision of the detailing at the corners allows a sense of openness, despite the raw strength of the steel and concrete structural elements.

1 Un espace à peindre.
2 Entre la maison et la colline, l'espace protégé et intime apporte un plus à la géométrie de la maison.
3–5 La précision du détail des angles donne un sentiment d'ouverture malgré l'aspect brut des éléments de structure en acier et béton.

1 Raum zum Malen.
2 Zwischen Haus und Hang schafft die Geometrie nebenbei einen geschützten, privaten Raum.
3–5 Die präzise Detailarbeit an den Ecken vermittelt ein Gefühl der Offenheit, ungeachtet der massiven Stärke von Stahl und Beton.

5

Entrance level plan

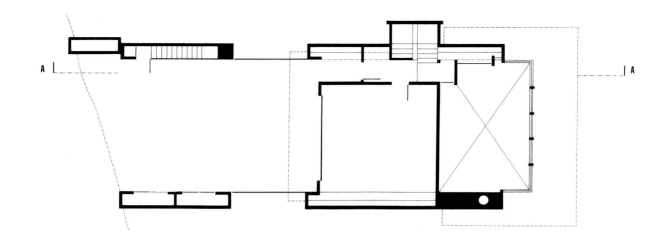

Middle floor plan

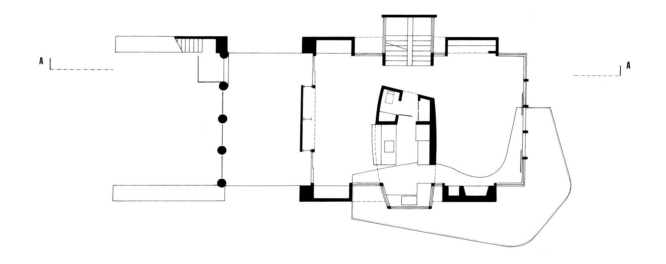

Lower floor plan

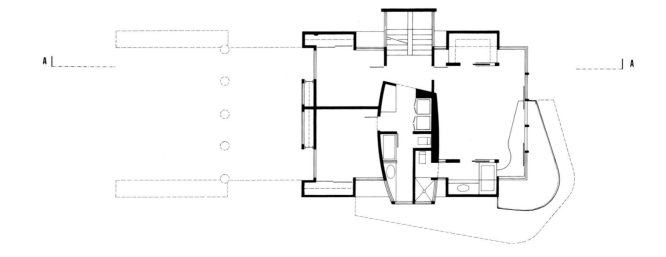

section A–A

Philip Banta & Associates
Architecture
1993
Address 43 Perth Place, Oakland CA
Client David and Lisa Shaw
Design Philip Banta
Project manager Philip Hyndman
General contractor Challenge Construction
(Bob Whitaker)
Structural engineer Wes Ogawa Associates
Size 4000 square feet
Cost US$550,000

XYZ House

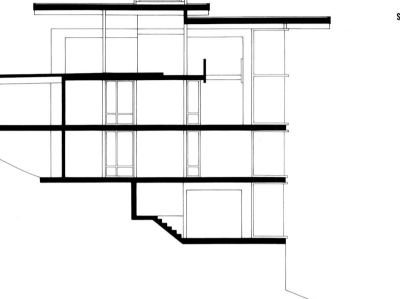

Site plan

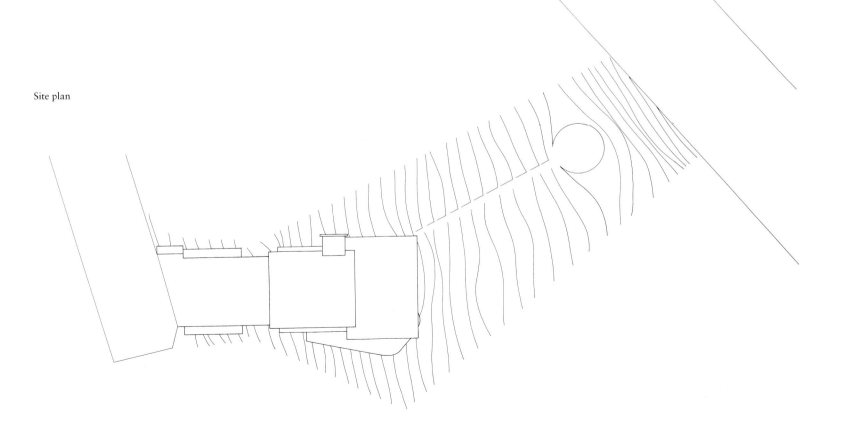

House on a Hilltop
Mark Horton /
Architecture

This house makes a powerful statement. It stands unapologetically on the peak of a hill, rising above its neighbours to give unparalleled views of the South Bay, San Francisco and the Bay and Golden Gate bridges.

Two discrete volumes positioned next to one another are linked by a glass and metal connector. The two objects are characterised by the tautness and density of their skin, a cement-board panel, and the precise definition of their edges. These cubic forms are then punctured by a separate system of metal and glass balconies, bays and a prominent skylight. The dense skin reads as a base against which the lighter protruding elements appear as sub-objects of the composition.

The building's simple forms are subtly made less than perfect: the roof of the main volume is asymmetrical; the skylight is awkwardly pointed; the balconies are irregular.

The house has views through at every level, but it is also a house that looks at itself. Horton has limited direct exposure to the dramatic views over the Bay to those areas which tend to be more contemplative in nature; the main functional areas – kitchen, family room and so on – look on to a courtyard and only indirectly on to the Bay. One of the most appealing elements in the design is a small window – hardly more than a foot square – set into the wall of one of the living rooms. This frames the view like a

landscape painting and has a magnetic power to draw the eye, a demonstration of the power of control.

Mark Horton: 'How has this house affected the family which occupies it? Perhaps an easier question to answer would be how it has not affected them. It has not affected them in the same way as their English Tudor house, which burned down in the fire, did – it has not left them with the daily impression that the nineteenth century is alive and well in the last decade of the twentieth; it has not left them with the idea that human progress stopped at a point at which steamships were the basic mode of transportation; it has not left them with the idea that technology is bad and

craft is good and that the two are inherently separate.

'This house has attempted to be a comfortable, warm and livable home created in the last decade of the second millennium. This house has attempted to show that rational utilisation of space and surfaces can create an enjoyable place to live without the unneeded decoration of past generations. And this house has attempted to provide an optimistic view of the continued progress of technology and science.'

1–3 A house on a hill: standing above its neighbours, the House on a Hilltop provides its owners with views of the South Bay, San Francisco, the Bay Bridge and the Golden Gate. Inhabitants of the Oakland Hills have been granted views of the house.

1–3 La maison sur une colline surplombant ses voisines offre à ses résidents et propriétaires une vue sur la Baie sud de San Francisco et les ponts de la Baie et du Golden Gate. Les habitants de Oakland Hills ont l'avantage d'avoir une vue sur la maison.

1–3 Ein Haus am Berg. Hoch über seinen Nachbarn eröffnet das »House on a Hilltop« der Familie den Blick auf die South Bay, San Francisco, die Bay-Brücke und die Golden-Gate-Brücke. Das Haus wurde für die Bewohner von Oakland Hills zur Besichtigung geöffnet.

1

Dieses Haus gibt ein eindrucksvolles Statement ab. Es steht dreist auf einer Bergspitze, ragt hoch über die Nachbarhäuser hinaus und gewährt einen unvergleichlichen Ausblick auf die South Bay, San Francisco, die Bay-Brücke und die Golden-Gate-Brücke.

Zwei getrennte, nebeneinanderstehende Abschnitte werden durch ein Verbindungsstück aus Glas und Metall gekoppelt. Das Charakteristische an den zwei Objekten ist die Straffheit und Dichte ihrer Außenhaut aus Zementplatten sowie die Präzision und Schärfe der Kanten. Diese kubischen Formen werden durch ein separates System von Metall- und Glasbalkonen, Erkern und einem auffälligen Dachfenster aufgelockert. Die dichte Außenhaut wirkt wie

ein Hintergrund, auf dem die leichteren, hervorstehenden Elemente wie untergeordnete Kompositionsobjekte erscheinen. Die schlichten Formen des Gebäudes bergen subtile Unvollkommenheiten: Das Dach des Hauptvolumens ist asymmetrisch; das Dachfenster hat einen ungünstigen Winkel; die Balkone widersetzen sich der Norm.

Auf jeder Ebene öffnet sich das Haus dem Durchblick, aber andererseits ist es auch ein Haus der Selbstbetrachtung. Horton erschließt das imposante Panorama der Bucht uneingeschränkt nur in solchen Bereichen, die eher kontemplativen Charakter haben; die wichtigsten Funktionsräume – Küche, Gemeinschaftsraum usw. – blicken auf einen Innenhof

und nur indirekt auf die Bucht. Zu den attraktivsten Elementen des Entwurfs zählt ein kleines Fenster – nur knapp 30 x 30 cm groß – das in die Mauer eines der Wohnzimmer eingelassen wurde. Es rahmt den Ausblick ein wie ein Landschaftsgemälde und zieht wie ein Magnet das Auge an – ein Beweis für die Macht der Beherrschung.

Mark Horton: »Wie sich das Haus auf die Familie ausgewirkt hat, die darin wohnt? Vielleicht läßt sich eine andere Frage leichter beantworten, nämlich: Wie hat es sich nicht ausgewirkt? Es hat einen anderen Effekt als das frühere, abgebrannte Haus im englischen Tudorstil – es vermittelt ihr nicht jeden Tag den Eindruck, daß das 19. Jahrhundert im letzten

2

Cette maison est chargée de sens. Elevée avec impertinence sur le haut d'une colline, elle dépasse ses voisines et offre une vue imprenable sur la Baie sud de San Francisco et les ponts de la Baie et du Golden Gate.

Deux volumes discrets, placés l'un à côté de l'autre, sont reliés par une unité de raccord en verre et métal. Les deux éléments se distinguent par la tension et l'épaisseur de leur peau faite de panneaux de ciment, et par la pureté de leurs angles. Ces formes cubiques sont ponctuées par un système indépendant de balcons en verre et métal, de travées et de tabatières spectaculaires. La peau épaisse délimite la base et par contraste donne un aspect léger aux éléments qui dépassent

comme s'ils étaient des objets secondaires de la composition. Les formes simples de la construction sont conçues avec certaines imperfections : le toit du volume principal est asymétrique, les tabatières sont orientées maladroitement et les lignes des balcons sont irrégulières.

La maison offre à chaque niveau une vue sur l'extérieur tout en portant un regard sur elle-même. Horton a limité les ouvertures directes sur la vue spectaculaire de la Baie pour favoriser celles qui sont d'une nature plus contemplative. Les espaces fonctionnels, tels que la cuisine, le salon, etc., donnent sur une cour ainsi que sur la Baie mais de façon indirecte. Un des détails les plus attrayants dans la conception de cette maison est une toute

petite fenêtre (d'environ 30 sur 30 cm) insérée dans le mur d'un des salons qui encadre une vue semblable à une peinture de paysage et attire le regard comme un aimant – une belle démonstration de la maîtrise de l'espace.

Mark Horton : «Quel effet cette maison a-t-elle sur la famille qui y habite ? Peut-être serait-il plus simple de se demander quels sont les effets qu'elle ne produit pas. Elle n'agit pas de la même manière que leur précédente maison, de style Tudor, qui a brûlé lors de l'incendie. Elle ne dégage pas en permanence cette impression que le XIXème siècle est encore présent en cette fin de siècle. Elle ne leur donne pas le sentiment que le progrès de la civilisation s'est arrêté au moment où les paquebots

étaient le moyen de transport élémentaire. Elle ne leur donne pas le sentiment que la technologie est une mauvaise chose et l'artisanat une bonne chose et que chacun d'eux est intrinsèquement distinct de l'autre.

L'objectif a été de réaliser une maison qui soit confortable, chaleureuse et habitable et conçue dans l'esprit qui anime la dernière décennie du XXème siècle. Avec cette maison, on a tenté de démontrer que l'utilisation rationnelle de l'espace et des surfaces crée un lieu qui est agréable à vivre, et ce sans la décoration superflue des générations précédentes. Enfin, cette maison a tenté de présenter une vue optimiste sur le progrès de la technologie et des sciences».

Jahrzehnt des 20. noch quicklebendig und aktuell ist; es hat ihr nicht suggeriert, daß die Menschheit seit der Zeit, als sie auf Dampfschiffe angewiesen war, keine Fortschritte mehr gemacht hat; es hat sie nicht glauben gemacht, daß Technologie schlecht und Handwerk gut ist und daß beide im Prinzip nichts miteinander zu tun haben.

Dieses Haus soll ein gemütliches, warmes und bewohnbares Zuhause sein, das im letzten Jahrzehnt des zweiten Jahrtausends entstanden ist. Das Haus soll zeigen, daß man durch die rationale Nutzung von Raum und Fläche einen attraktiven Wohnraum schaffen kann, der des unnötigen Schmuckwerks vergangener Generationen nicht bedarf. Und das Haus

soll eine optimistische Haltung zu dem laufenden technologischen und wissenschaftlichen Fortschritt zum Ausdruck bringen.«

3

1–3 Two distinct volumes clad in cement board and connected by a glass and metal element make up the house.

4–7 The taut skin of the house is repeatedly punctured by a series of metal and glass balconies, bays, and an over-scale skylight.

1–3 Deux volumes distincts revêtus de panneaux de ciment et reliés entre eux par un élément de verre et de métal qui donne à la maison son unité.

4–7 La peau tendue est régulièrement ponctuée par une série de balcons en verre et métal, de voûtes et d'immenses tabatières.

1–3 Zwei getrennte, mit Betonplatten verkleidete Volumen werden durch ein Verbindungsstück aus Glas und Metall zu einem Ganzen gekoppelt.

4–7 Die straffe Außenhaut wird immer wieder durch eine Reihe von Metall- und Glasbalkonen, Erkern und ein auffälliges Dachfenster aufgelockert.

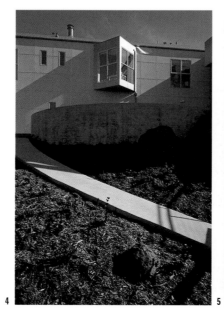

6

7

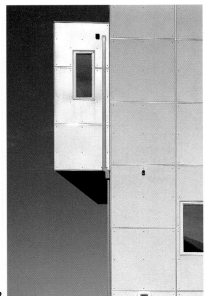

1–3 Close up, the barn-like appearance
of the house vanishes as
complexity becomes apparent.
 4 The language of glass and
aluminium brought into the space
between the two volumes.
 5 The house looks out, and in on
itself – another confident gesture

1–3 En se rapprochant, l'aspect de
grange de la maison disparaît au
fur et à mesure que la complexité
devient apparente.
 4 Le langage du verre et de
l'aluminium dans l'espace entre
les deux volumes.
 5 La maison offre une vue sur
l'extérieur tout en portant un
regard sur elle-même.

1–3 Beim näheren Hinsehen wird der
Eindruck von einer Scheune durch
Komplexität abgelöst.
 4 Die Sprache von Glas und
Aluminium erfüllt den Raum
zwischen den beiden Volumen.
 5 Das Haus geht sowohl aus sich
heraus als auch in sich – ein
weiterer Ausdruck des
Selbstbewußtseins.

4

5

1

1 Views of the distant landscape
take in the house as well.
2–4 Light-filled interiors, with volumes
closely controlled to provide
comfort.

1 La vue du paysage, qui s'étend
sur des kilomètres, fait partie
intégrante de la maison.
2–4 Les intérieurs inondés de lumière
dont les volumes sont maîtrisés
avec brio donnent un sentiment de
bien-être.

1 Auch beim weiten Ausblick ist
das Haus mit der Landschaft
verbunden.
2–4 Lichtüberflutete Innenräume, im
Volumen behaglich kontrolliert.

2

3

4

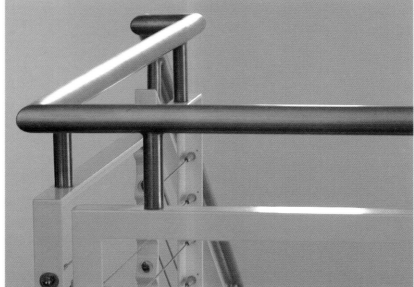

1–2 Staircase details.
3–5 How to control a view: a frame in a place of transition.
6–7 The gallery on the upper floor is an outbreak of linearity.

1–2 Détail d'escalier.
3–5 Comment contrôler la vue : un cadre à un endroit de transition.
6–7 La galerie de l'étage supérieur est une explosion de linéarité.

1–2 Treppendetails.
3–5 Gezielter Ausblick: Rahmen an einem Ort der Rastlosigkeit.
6–7 Die Galerie im Obergeschoß ist ein Ausbruch der Linearität.

6

7

1 An interior for the end of the century.
2 Junior bedroom.
3 Enclosure and transparency in the bathroom echo the language of the exterior.
4–5 Lying beneath the massive skylight in the master bedroom provides changing views of clouds and stars.

1 Un intérieur pour la fin de ce siècle.
2 Chambre d'enfant.
3 L'espace fermé et transparent de la salle de bains rappelle le vocabulaire de l'extérieur.
4–5 Allongé sous les immenses tabatières de la chambre des parents, on peut voir les nuages et les étoiles.

1 Ein Interieur für das ausklingende Jahrhundert.
2 Kinderschlafzimmer.
3 Umfassung und Transparenz im Badezimmer sprechen die Sprache des Exterieurs.
4–5 Liegt man unter dem gewaltigen Dachfenster des Hauptschlafzimmers, sieht man Wolken und Sterne in ihrem Wechselspiel vorüberziehen.

4

5

Lower floor plan

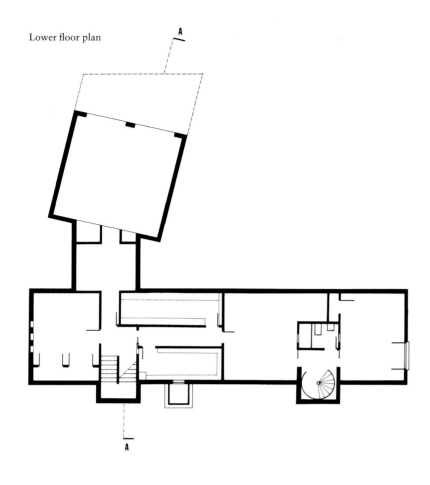

Top floor plan

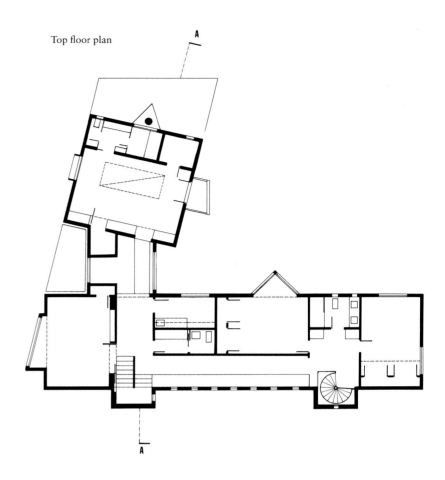

Ground floor plan

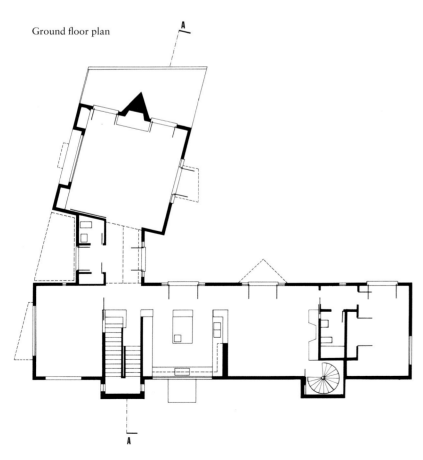

Mark Horton / Architecture
1995

Design team Mark Horton, David Yum
General contractor Marrone Brothers, Inc
Structural consultant Structural Design Engineers
Lighting consultant Becca Foster Lighting Design
Size 4500 square feet

section A–A

Site plan

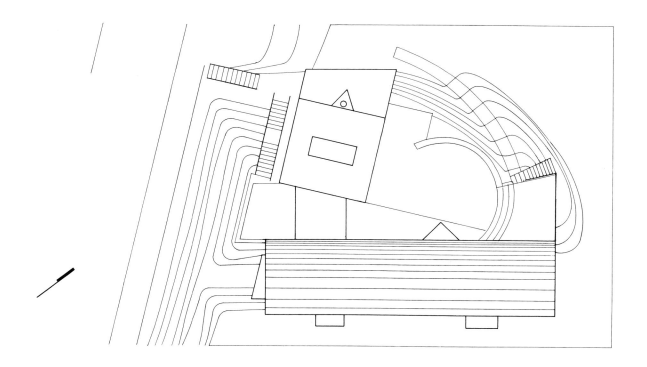

Stanley Saitowitz

Born 1949

Education University of Witwatersrand, South Africa, graduated 1975; University of California, Berkeley, graduated 1977

Work Eliot Noyes professor, Harvard Graduate School of Design 1991–2; Bruce Goff professor, University of Oaklahoma 1993; has taught at Southern California Institute of Architecture, UCLA, University of Texas, University of Witwatersrand, South Africa; established current practice in South Africa 1975

Major projects House at Halfway House, Transvaal, South Africa 1977
Quady Winery, Madera CA 1983
California Museum of Photography, Riverside 1986
Di Napoli House, Los Gatos CA 1987
McDonald House, Stinson Beach CA 1987
AGB Library Competition, Berlin, Germany 1988
Natoma Street Live/Work, San Francisco CA 1989
Byron Meyer House, Napa CA 1989
Nine structures, Mill Race Park, Columbus IN 1990
Rabin Residence, Tiburon CA 1991
Holocaust Memorial, Boston MA 1991
San Francisco Embarcadero Promenade CA 1991
Theodore Hullar House, Davis CA 1991
Adelie Bischoff House, Oakland CA 1992
Lesser House, Berkeley CA 1992
Richard Barnes House and Studio, San Francisco CA 1992
Capp Street project, San Francisco CA 1993
Thousand Oaks Elementary School, CA 1994
Rosenthal/Murphy Residence, Berkeley CA 1994
Berkeley Public Safety Building competition, CA 1995

Prizes San Francisco Arts Achievement Award 1996

Exhibitions 'Geological Architecture', Walker Art Center, Minneapolis MN 1990

Publications *Architectural Review* (2/88); *The Harvard Architectural Review* (8/93); *Architecture* (8/95); Kenneth Frampton, David Larkin, *American Masterworks: The Twentieth Century House*, Rizzoli 1995; George Wagner (ed), *Stanley Saitowitz: A House in the Transvaal*, Princeton Architectural Press 1996; Stanley Saitowitz, *Stanley Saitowitz: Architecture at Rice 33*, Princeton Architectural Press 1996

Jim Jennings

Born 1940

Education UC Berkeley, graduated 1966

Work SOM San Francisco CA; established current practice 1986

Major projects 25 Brush Place, San Francisco CA 1989
Barclay Simpson Sculpture Studio, California College of Arts and Crafts 1991
Mausoleums, Italian Cemetery 1991 and 1997; masterplan (unbuilt) 1992
Copas-Holland Residence, Oakland CA 1994
Bayview Richmond Properties, Richmond CA 1996
Gandia Stephenson Residence, Calistoga CA 1996
Kane Residence, Ross CA 1996
Oliver Residence, San Francisco CA 1996

Publications *GA Houses* (30 and 31/91); *Progressive Architecture* (1/92); *California Country*, ChronicleBooks 1992; *DBZ* (2/94); *Zodiac* (3/94); *GA Houses* (46/95); *Architecture* (8/95)

Biographies

Philip Banta

Born 1950
Education Harvard University, graduated 1972; UC Berkeley, graduated 1978
Work Lecturer UC Berkeley 1978–9; visiting critic University of Texas at Austin 1979; founded and ran mentor programme, Emery High, Emeryville CA 1989-94; Zimmer, Gunsul, Frasca, Portland OR 1973-4; SOM San Francisco CA 1974-5; BETA Inc (Building and Energy Technical Analysis), Emeryville CA 1978–; established current practice 1978
Major projects Senator Alquist State Office Building, San Jose CA 1980
Hollis Street Project Building, Emeryville CA 1983
Colors Restaurant, Emeryville CA 1983
California Department of Health office interiors, Emeryville CA 1984
Salvet French Clothing Boutique, San Francisco CA 1986
Tzintzuntzan headquarters, Berkeley CA 1986
House at Stinson Beach, CA 1987
Magnolia Court live/work complex, Oakland CA 1988
WSU Agri-tech building and masterplan, Pullman WA 1989
MicroAnalytical laboratory interiors, Emeryville CA 1989
Monterey Boulevard housing development, Oakland CA 1989
Tiburon 'B' Radius House, Tiburon CA 1990
Polymer Technologies laboratory interiors, Emeryville CA 1991
Chabot Canyon Racquet Club, Oakland CA 1992
Global Business Network office interiors, Emeryville CA 1993
Royal Coffee headquarters, Emeryville CA 1995
Pocket Building live/work building, Oakland CA 1996
Cook Cabin, Soda Springs CA 1996
Publications *Progressive Architecture* (1/82); *Architecture* (10/89); *Architectural Record* (6/90); *Builder* (10/92)

Mark Horton

Born 1956
Education Dartmouth College; Harvard Graduate School of Design
Work Adjunct professor California College of Arts and Crafts; lecturer, UC at Berkeley; visiting design critic University of Arkansas, Boston Architectural Center, University of North Carolina; co-founder 2AES: the Art and Architecture Exhibition Space; SOM San Francisco CA; Backen, Arrigoni, and Ross Architects, San Francisco CA; established current practice 1986
Major projects Godry Residence, San Francisco CA 1990
McCrary Residence, Hillsborough CA 1991
Hearst Residence, Ridgway CO 1991
Healdsburg Residence, Healdsburg CA 1991
Steffen Residence, Oakland CA 1994
Tansey/Greenfield Residence, Oakland CA 1995
The Little School, San Francisco CA 1995
Good Samaritan Family Resource Center and Housing, San Francisco CA 1996
Market Street housing, San Francisco CA 1996
Operation Starcross (HIV/AIDS hospice for children), Constanta, Romania
Prizes *SF Magazine* 'Best of Bay' Design Award 1990; *Northern California Home and Garden* Design Achievement Award 1992; Architectural Delineation Award, AIA/SF Computer Forum 1993; Young Architects Award, *Progressive Architecture* 1993; Architectural Abstract Rendering Award, AIA/SF Computer Forum 1994; awarded Aga Khan Fellowship to document indigenous architecture of Republic of Mali, Africa

Exhibitions 'New Architecture in the Oakland Hills', Limn Gallery, San Francisco CA; 'Mud' (photography of Sahelian architecture), Limn Gallery, San Francisco CA; 'Islamic Vernacular', AIA Gallery, San Francisco CA
Publications *DBZ* (10/92); *Progressive Architecture* (7/93); *Häuser* (3/94)

●●●ellipsis

ellipsis specialises in publishing contemporary architecture and art and culture using a range of media, from books to the world wide web. Contact us for a copy of our pocket catalogue.

… earthier than Racine, more passionate than Stendhal, more encyclopaedic than Diderot and saucier than Escoffier.

Hermine Poitou, INIT

A: 55 Charlotte Road London EC2A 3QT
E: …@ellipsis.co.uk
W: http://www.ellipsis.co.uk/ellipsis
T: +44 171 739 3157
F: +44 171 739 3175

●●●electric editions

The ellipsis world wide web site is growing. It has been presented at numerous exhibitions and festivals, and the critics like it:

ellipsis wins. It wins with creativity. It wins with content. It wins with innovation. You need to see this site, just to get a glimpse of what online publishing can do. The overall design pulls the surfer in and, with its intriguing graphical concepts, almost demands that s/he stick around for a while … Users cruise through ellipsis pointing and clicking at icons that don't seem to make sense at first, since they rely heavily on intuitive action. But users 'learn by doing' what the different symbols and metaphors mean. It's a little complicated, but also challenging. The results are a joy to see.

This is quite possibly one of the greatest web sites I have ever visited: ever-unfolding into interactive activity, a hyperlink game, and digital transcendence. This IS the place to be.

BG, The Net magazine (USA)

The electric art cd-rom/book series was launched in March with Simon Biggs' *Book of Shadows*; number 2, *Passagen*, is due in Spring 97.

●●●paper editions

Our intention is always to publish in the most appropriate format – ranging from the interactive, intangible on-line pages of the world wide web, to the dual electronic and paper form of the electric art series, *Mekons United* with its book and audio cd, and conventional books.

These include Architecture in Context, books designed to appeal to anyone with an interest in contemporary building. The first four titles cover recent projects in Tokyo, Las Vegas, San Francisco, and Vienna. Essays provide the context necessary to understand the work – antecedents, functions, technology, urban issues – which is shown in specially commissioned photographs and drawings.

We have a paperback reprint of our very successful autobiography of Peter Rice, *An Engineer Imagines*, and a ground-breaking and very beautiful book on architecture and cyberspace, *Digital Dreams*. *The Internet and Everyone* is an important work by John Chris Jones, author of *Design Methods* and *Designing Designing*, in which he brings an unparalleled depth and range of thought to the information superhighway. Starting life on the internet, one stage of the work's development will be its existence as a book.

●●●architecture guides

The best new guides to recent architecture are published by ellipsis.

Colin Amery, The Financial Times

With a critical approach, an innovative, pocket-sized format, high-quality illustrations, and award-winning design, this series of guides – now available in English, German and French editions – describes and comments on significant contemporary architecture.

In preparation are books covering New York, San Francisco, Paris, Berlin, Sydney, Dublin, Madrid, Istanbul, Budapest, and Hong Kong, with still more to come.

Chicago: a guide to recent architecture

Susanna Sirefman

… should proved irresistible to architecture buffs.

Chicago Herald Tribune

… the perfect yuppie travel companion … discrete enough to refer to on the Loop, potted enough to do so between stops, detailed enough to impress and indiscrete enough to entertain.

The Art Book Review Quarterly

England: a guide to recent architecture

Samantha Hardingham/photographs by Susan Benn

Latest in a delectable series … informative, opinionated, critical text; compact, sharply printed pix. Hardingham is a positive guide to the grand, the witty, the shoddy, the soaring, the sober, the dumb.

The Observer

… remarkably up-to-date … a fresh perspective is provided in the concise and spikily perceptive comments from the AA-trained author. The book is a pocket-sized bonus for the architecture-watcher.

Paul Finch, The Architects' Journal

London: a guide to recent architecture

Samantha Hardingham

… positively plump with exploring zeal and opinion … Truly pocket-sized and strongly recommended.

The Observer

… it can only be applauded for broadening the audience for contemporary architecture and design.

Lorenzo Apicella, Building Design

Las Vegas: a guide to recent architecture

Frances Anderton and John Chase/photographs by Keith Collie

This is the first guide to the architecture of Las Vegas. It describes and illustrates the casinos, the hotels, and the glorious lights and neon signage of the most popular gambling mecca in the world.

Los Angeles: a guide to recent architecture

Dian Phillips-Pulverman

In the second half of this century Greater Los Angeles has become a forcing ground for avant-garde architecture, and the appetite for experiment is as strong as ever. This book describes and illustrates more than 100 buildings completed over the last ten years.

Prague: a guide to twentieth-century architecture

Ivan Margolius/photographs by Keith Collie

… up-to-date and well worth reading … An excellent small (in size), big (in content) guide which should decorate the shelf, or rather the pocket, of any interested architect.

Robert Voticky, Building Design

Tokyo: a guide to recent architecture

Noriyuki Tajima/photographs by Keith Collie

… beautifully designed and illustrated … Tajima's witty and enticing commentaries entice readers to make their own journeys of discovery.

Joe LaPenta, The Daily Yomiuri

Vienna: a guide to recent architecture

Ingerid Helsing Almaas/photographs by Keith Collie

… that rarity – a guide-book that is a pleasure to read in full.

The Architects' Journal

Mekons United

The Mekons were one of a group of bands to emerge from Leeds University/art school in the late 1970s. In the years since, the band has moved from punk through various musical styles, collaborated with dancers, artists and writers, and produced a stream of albums. In April 1996 an exhibition of Mekons art opened in Florida. This book presents a selection of that art, and includes a major essay by Terry Atkinson on the pop art explosion and the politics that led to punk, other essays on the economics of rock 'n' roll, the topography of Leeds, football and popular culture, art theory, and on the Mekons themselves.

The book also includes extracts from *Living in Sin*, the Mekons' novel in progress, with contributions from Kathy Acker, and a cd with more than an hour of previously unreleased Mekons music.

Mekons United is a *tour de force* from perhaps the only band that exhibits equal ability in the musical and visual arts

Chris Morris, Billboard

Digital Dreams: architecture and cyberspace

Neil Spiller

Architecture in crisis: the era of virtual reality, cyberspace, prosthetics and nano-technology. **Secrecy and experimentation – the fears and ecstasies of the painter; the drawing as a recording of the body's creative dance.** Exploring superspace as a series of perceptual frames or surfaces with intersecting boundaries. **Surface empathy is one of the conditions of being human.** Cyberspace is another realm of architectural opportunity. **Alchemy and its transformations parallel the emergent technologies of cyberspace, nano-technology and prosthetics.** The concept of the quantum smear (the ubiquity of the electron) leads to the idea of parallel universes and the infinite states of the object.

An Engineer Imagines

Peter Rice

Now in paperback, Peter Rice's autobiography is a personal account of the joy and enthusiasm he gave to and took from his profession. Rice was widely acclaimed as the greatest structural engineer of his generation, a man who, in Renzo Piano's words, could design structures 'like a pianist who can play with his eyes shut'.

The book explains Rice's perception of, and contribution to, his most significant projects and lets the reader discover his very genuine humanity and concern for quality and sensuality. All concerned with these issues in our built environment should take the trouble to read it.

Ian Ritchie, The Architects' Journal

In *An Engineer Imagines*, the author accomplishes what was surely his principal reason for devoting his last year to this book: making vivid the process, excitement, and satisfactions of creative engineering.

Joseph Passonneuau, Architectural Record

Britain: a guide to architectural styles from 1066 to the present

Hubert Pragnell

I have a friend who once asked for a list of architectural styles to pin up in her bathroom so that she could recite them every day as she prepared for the world. She worried that she did not know when the Romanesque ended and the Gothic began. Even more worrying for some is knowing what is going on in contemporary architecture. For instance, what is post-modernism all about?

At last help is at hand … Above all, this little book is for the beginner to take to the streets. Armed with its basics, they may find enough architectural pleasure to last a lifetime.

Colin Amery, The Financial Times

The Art of the Structural Engineer

Bill Addis

Recognition of the structural engineer's contribution to building design has grown enormously in recent years. Rather than being seen as a sobering influence on the creativity of architects, daring and innovative engineers are rightly acknowledged as creators in their own right, exploring materials and structures as part of the design team.

Engineers who read this book will come to understand architects better. It will help architects too, even if only to look at engineers in a kinder light.

Will Howie, New Civil Engineer

The Internet and Everyone

John Chris Jones

how to improve the world without making matters worse
this is the architecture of living decentrally
:prelude:
Is there something that can be added now to the idea of the internet, and to its presence, that really improves industrial life, and culture?
My first answer to this question, which I wrote as an outline of this book for ellipsis and McGraw Hill, was as follows:
…

Date Wed, 25 Oct 1995 02:07:19 +0100
To …@ellipsis.co.uk
From jcj@ellipsis.co.uk
Subject the internet & everyone

dear tom & jonathan … & everyone
OUTLINE OF THE IDEAS
When I think of the internet I realise that, though beginning as a special medium additional to others such as surface mail, phone, fax, radio, tv, etc, it is likely to grow rapidly as a general or meta-medium (as was print and the book) that legitimises and changes the forms of all the others.

What I will be writing is my long-held view that, as computation expands, all of the specialised departments of modern life, everything from government and education to medicine and show business, will have to undergo gradual but total change or transformation as the computernet and its possibilities, threatening and benign, provoke organisations and ordinary people to develop in extraordinary ways, many of them contradictory.

That is, I will suggest that there will evolve computernet-based versions of everything, very different from the present ones (which are based on the direct presence of people in specialised roles).

The central point of this view of things is that specialisation is no longer the right form for living in industrial culture. I believe that the logic of the change from mechanical to post-mechanical, via electronic media and computing, implies that people cease to organise themselves in specialised roles, as experts highly skilled in narrowband jobs. With the aid of a computerised internet, everyone should be able to take back (from what remains of the specialised professions) the creativeness and initiative that was long ago lost to them. As I see it, the presence of accessible computing power, embedded in everything, will turn the technical know-how of experts into accessible software and their manual skills and intuitions into the normal abilities of everyone else.

The obvious precedent for this is in the early days of writing and printing. Where once there were expert scribes and readers, able to write and to print what most people could only speak, there is now widespread literacy and the recent coming of self-publishing, by computer desk-top.

Equally relevant to this is the way in which the highly complex skills of speaking and listening to colloquial speech, still beyond the abilities of computers, are not beyond the immense abilities of every single person, the gifts we were all born with. And also the way in which languages grow and change spontaneously, in ways which baffle the so-called experts in language, but without any trace of central control or design or rule by specialists.

I believe that in the immediate future of the internet the question of whether it is to grow decentrally as it began, or under the central control which the media people and the corporations would like it to become, is a main question of the time. To me, nothing else matters as much, though I suppose that is crankiness, or fanaticism. (We have to go beyond that if the future is not to be a mess!)

My purpose in writing the book is to show in some detail exactly how it is that the old path (of expert centralism) is no longer right and that the new path (of what has been called creative democracy made possible by computernet) is the right way to go. Just because it's more human, in a way that primitive industrialism never was.

In this vision of universal change from centralism to its reverse, one or two things are essential: for example, how to let go and how to keep the centre empty.

But I've not got time at the moment to say any more than that.